# THE LIVING TOGETHER KIT

by Attorneys Toni Ihara & Ralph Warner

Research Associate: Sarah Weisman

 ▪ 950 Parker Street, Berkeley, CA 94710

Nolo Press is committed to keeping its books up-to-date. Each new printing, whether or not it is called a new edition, has been completely revised to reflect latest law changes. This book was reprinted and updated on the last date indicated below. If this book is out-of-date, do not rely on the information without checking it in a new edition.

| | |
|---|---|
| First Edition (Sex, Living Together & the Law) | 1974 |
| Second Printing | 1976 |
| Second Edition | 1978 |
| Third Edition | 1979 |
| Fawcett Editions | 1979, 1980 |
| German Edition | 1980 |
| Fourth Edition | 1984 |

| | |
|---|---|
| *Editor:* | Leslie Ihara Armistead |
| *Production Director:* | Keija Kimura |
| *Book Design and Lay-out:* | Toni Ihara |
| *Illustrations:* | Linda Allison |
| *Illustrations:* | Root Brague |

ISBN 0-917316-73-8

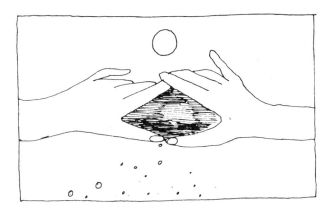

## A LITTLE HISTORY

Carmen Massey and Ralph Warner co-authored the original legal guide for un-married couples in 1974. It was entitled *Sex, Living Together And The Law* and was a successful and well-received book. In 1976 just as a new edition was being planned Carmen died. Her death was a severe blow to all who knew her: she was truly a person who gave more than she received, and whose light and good energy made her loved by many.

It wasn't until 1978 that those of us at Nolo Press felt clear enough to go on with revisions for the book. By this time *Sex, Living Together And The Law* was hopelessly out-of-date and it was necessary to create a new book. However, some of Carmen's original excellent work was still topical and an arrangement was made with her estate to include it in the new book. We feel good that some of our friend's positive ideas and common sense are still available to help people.

### AND A BIG THANK YOU

Many old friends, and a few new ones, helped us make this a better book. We would particularly like to thank Linda Allison, Leslie Armistead, David Brown, Keija Kimura, Walter Warner and Sarah Weisman. Special thanks to Gary Kitajo and Ron Lomax whose kind assistance has made doing research almost a pleasure.

## ABOUT NOLO

Nolo Press consists of a group of people (some lawyers, some not) who came to see much of what passes for the practice of law as being mumbo jumbo and paper shuffling designed by lawyers to mystify and confuse. Acting from the conviction "that there must be a better way", we have committed ourselves to trying to liberate the legal system from lawyers. A sane society needs a dispute resolution procedure that is cheap, fast, easy-to-understand and which is accessible to all.

Started in 1971 with *How To Do Your Own Divorce*, Nolo Press has become a positive energy force for people who want to open up our legal system and make its so-called trade secrets available to all. Nolo has now published a dozen books aimed at providing people with the information necessary to help themselves. In the process, it has helped the authors to maintain their own self-respect in a field where bank balances have often been more prominent than ethics.

Our books have been written, illustrated, designed and printed by a group of friends headquartered in Berkeley and Occidental, California. Without ever planning to, we have created our own cottage industry. We hope you get as much out of reading this book as we did in making it, and we would be delighted to get any feedback you would care to send our way.

# Contents

| | |
|---|---|
| **INTRODUCTION** | **9** |
| **CHAPTER 1 — LIVING TOGETHER: OLD WINE IN A NEW GLASS** | **11** |
| **CHAPTER 2 — SEX, LIVING TOGETHER AND THE LAW** | **16** |
| A. DEFINITIONS | 16 |
| B. IF IT FEELS GOOD, IT MAY BE ILLEGAL | 17 |
| C. COMMON LAW MARRIAGE | 21 |
| **CHAPTER 3 — PRACTICAL ASPECTS OF LIVING TOGETHER** | **23** |
| A. GETTING TOGETHER | 23 |
| B. SHARING BANK ACCOUNTS | 26 |
| C. CHARGE ACCOUNTS AND BUYING ON TIME | 26 |
| D. HOW TO APPLY FOR CREDIT | 26 |
| E. CREDIT AND CREDIT AGENCIES | 27 |
| F. BUYING A MOTOR VEHICLE | 31 |
| G. TRAVEL | 31 |
| H. DISCRIMINATION IN EMPLOYMENT | 33 |
| I. PAYING YOUR TAXES | 34 |
| J. WELFARE, FOOD STAMPS, MEDI-CARE | 36 |
| K. SOCIAL SECURITY | 37 |
| L. INSURANCE | 38 |
| M. SERIOUS ILLNESS | 41 |
| N. MISCELLANEOUS RIGHTS & RESPONSIBILITIES | 43 |
| **CHAPTER 4 — LIVING TOGETHER CONTRACTS & THE LAW** | **44** |
| A. A LITTLE HISTORY | 44 |
| B. THE MARVIN CASE AND OTHERS | 45 |
| C. CONCLUSION | 47 |
| **CHAPTER 5 — CONTRACTS** | **49** |
| STEP 1 — MAKE YOUR AGREEMENT | 50 |
| STEP 2 — PUT IT IN WRITING | 50 |
| STEP 3 — DESIGN YOUR CONTRACT | 51 |
| A. FILL-IN LIVING TOGETHER CONTRACTS | 52 |
| B. SHORTFORM PROPERTY CONTRACTS | 54 |
| C. AGREEMENTS COVERING JOINTLY ACQUIRED ITEMS | 56 |
| D. AGREEMENTS COVERING JOINT PROJECTS | 58 |
| E. AGREEMENTS COVERING HOMEMAKER SERVICES | 59 |

F. AGREEMENTS COVERING HOUSEHOLD EXPENSES AND
   PERSONAL IDIOSYNCRASIES                                        61
G. AGREEMENT DESIGNED FOR STRUGGLING ARTISTS                     63
H. AGREEMENT FOR PEOPLE IN SCHOOL                                64
I. ENFORCEABILITY OF AGREEMENTS                                  65
I. MEDIATION & ARBITRATION OF DISPUTES                           66

**CHAPTER 6 — RENTING AND SHARING A HOME**                       69
A. RENTING A HOME                                                70
B. LEASES AND RENTAL AGREEMENTS                                  72
C. MOVING IN TOGETHER                                            74
D. MOVING INTO A FRIEND'S HOME                                   75
E. DEPOSITS                                                      82

**CHAPTER 7 — BUYING A HOUSE**                                   89
A. FINDING A HOUSE                                               90
B. FINANCING YOUR HOUSE                                          93
C. TAKING TITLE TO THE HOUSE                                    101
D. CONTRACTS BETWEEN UNMARRIED PEOPLE BUYING HOUSES             103

**CHAPTER 8 — STARTING A FAMILY**                               117
A. DECIDING TO HAVE A CHILD (OR ABORTION)                       117
B. NAMING THE BABY                                              119
C. PATERNITY                                                    120
D. LEGITIMACY                                                   122
E. PLANNING FOR SEPARATION                                      124
F. CUSTODY                                                      129
G. VISITATION                                                   130
H. ADOPTIONS                                                    130
I. SUPPORT OF AN ILLEGITIMATE CHILD                             133
J. BENEFITS FOR THE CHILD OF UNMARRIED PARENTS                  133
K. INHERITANCE RIGHTS OF AN ILLEGITIMATE CHILD                  134

**CHAPTER 9 — YOU AND YOUR PRIOR FAMILY**                       135
A. GETTING A DIVORCE WHILE LIVING WITH SOMEONE ELSE             135
B. CHILD CUSTODY                                                138
C. VISITATION OF CHILDREN                                       141
D. CHILD SUPPORT                                                142
E. SPOUSAL SUPPORT (ALIMONY)                                    145
F. DIVIDING THE PROPERTY                                        146
G. AFTER THE DIVORCE                                            147

**CHAPTER 10 — MOVING ON — DIVIDING THINGS**                    150
A. ON BEING HUMAN                                               150
B. PROPERTY                                                     152
C. PATERNITY                                                    153

D.  SUPPORT FOR DEPENDENTS     **153**
E.  SUPPORT FOR ONE ANOTHER     **155**
F.  CUSTODY OF CHILDREN     **156**

**CHAPTER 11 — DEATH**     **158**
A.  INHERITANCE RIGHTS OF UNMARRIED COUPLES     **158**
B.  DEFINITIONS     **159**
C.  INTESTATE SUCCESSION: WHAT HAPPENS TO YOUR PROPERTY IF
    YOU DIE WITHOUT A WILL?     **161**
D.  MAKING A WILL     **164**
E.  AVOIDING PROBATE     **167**
F.  AVOIDING DEATH TAXES     **169**
G.  PROVIDING FOR YOUR KIDS BY WILL     **169**
H.  DEATH AND LIVING TOGETHER CONTRACTS     **171**
I.  WHAT ABOUT MY BODY?     **172**

**CHAPTER 12 — LAWYERS AND HOW TO DEAL WITH THEM**     **174**
A.  LAW LIBRARIES     **175**
B.  WHEN DO YOU NEED A LAWYER?     **175**
C.  FINDING A LAWYER     **176**

**APPENDICES**     **179**

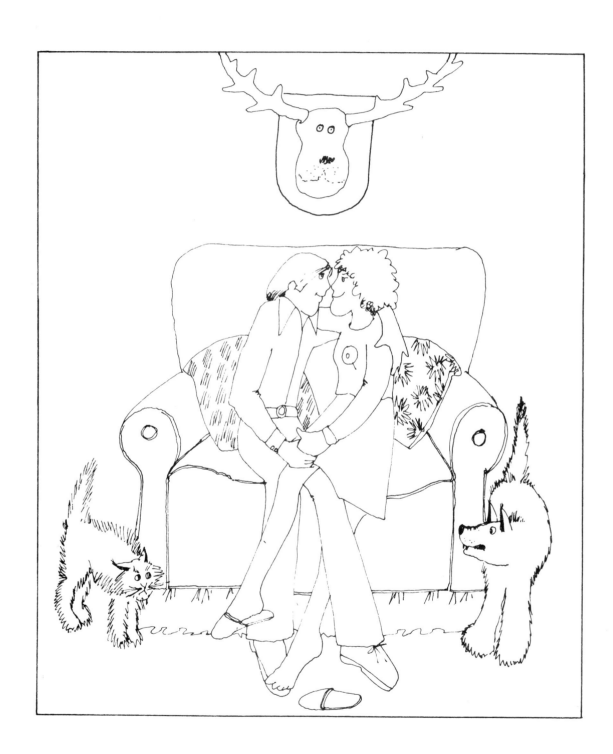

# ntroduction

The purpose of this book is to help unmarried heterosexual couples attain mutual understanding by presenting the legal rules surrounding living together in a way that will allow them to relax and stay in touch with their love for one another.* Our biases are toward simplicity and fairness.

Many people approach law as it relates to unmarried couples with hesitation, if not downright revulsion. Perhaps even the thought of introducing "unromantic" legal concepts into a personal relationship based on love and trust raises your hackles. And why not? The legal system as it now exists is commonly used in an aggressive attempt to screw every last nickel out of an adversary. Lawyers, some of whom have evolved no further than the hired guns of Dodge City, are the point men for a corrupt system having almost nothing to do with fairness, truth or the resolution of disputes.

We can't do much to change the legal system, but we can and do show you how existing rules can be used to sow the seeds of future understanding. Just as medicine need not be all pills and knives, law can be approached in a positive, conflict-avoiding way. We will show you that legal rules need not be incompatible with your best instincts and that law can be used creatively to minimize the possibility that your relationship will end in paranoia and bitterness.

Like it or not, there are many rules and regulations that apply to unmarried couples. You may ignore them for a time, but they are unlikely to ignore you. Once the rules are understood, the two of you will want to do some talking: to decide together

---

* Nolo Press also publishes *A Legal Guide for Lesbian & Gay Couples* by Hayden Curry and Denis Clifford. This is an extremely useful book which we heartily recommend. Because of this book, we do not attempt to meet the specific needs of gay and lesbian couples here.

how you and the rules can connect in a positive way. Then it will be typewriter time. We provide you with sample written agreements — living together contracts, real property agreements, wills, paternity statements, etc. It is up to you to adapt these samples to your needs. We advise you to write things down, not because we believe that most people are untrustworthy, but because we know from experience that over time, memories tend to blur. We ask you to make a small leap of faith and believe us when we tell you that sensible written agreements can do much to increase trust and harmony and that they are best made when you think that you will never need them, not when storm warnings are flying.

We believe that most unmarried couples can safely and easily master the great majority of the legal rules that affect them. We confess to our own hostility to what passes for justice in this country and to our bias against lawyers as a group. From time to time we do suggest that certain complicated situations necessitate a lawyer's advice, but you should know that there are doubtless many people who would advise you to rely on lawyers more often.

One point worthy of thought now, and as you read on, concerns the confusion of state laws relating to people living together. As you will learn or perhaps already know, law books are full of rules everyone, including the police, usually ignores. Ancient laws regulating who can sleep together, when and where, are a prime example. Many of you will find that in your daily living and loving arrangement you are technically law breakers, even though you are conducting your life in what you consider to be an ethical and practical way. Perhaps you will feel, as we do, that many of these laws need changing and will realize that change will come only if lots of people make their voices heard.

In writing this book we have had some trouble figuring out the best way to organize all the material, partly because laws are often overlapping and sometimes conflicting. But it is also because people approach life from so many different directions. One person is interested in buying a house with his partner of many years, while another wants to know whether living with someone can be used against her in a contested child custody case. Much information has been included, but perhaps not in the order you might have chosen. You will find the table of contents to be a good outline of the whole subject, as well as a direction finder for any individual problem. There is nothing difficult about the information we discuss, but now and then you may find some of the technical points a little sticky. So relax, take your time and make decisions only after you have read, and re-read the sections of interest to you.

# iving Together: Old Wine in a New Glass

When we wrote the first edition of this book, we dealt only with the legal and practical problems faced by unmarried couples. Living together itself seemed to us to be such a sensible, wholesome, easy way to live that we included no material on the emotional side of the relationship. As odd as it may seem, it never occurred to us that anyone still thought that unmarried couples were taking part in a controversial lifestyle. We simply didn't think that anyone would be interested in such questions as "Why do people choose to live together rather than get married?" or "What do you do or say when family members accuse you of living in sin?" or "How do you handle attacks from people whose narrow religious beliefs convince them that a woman who lives with a man is a prostitute?" or even "How do you introduce an unmarried couple at a party?" As it turned out, of course, we were very, very wrong.

We learned something about the narrowness of our own vision when we did a publicity tour following the publication of an earlier edition of this book. There we were on national television, prepared to recite all the legal do's and don't's that unmarried couples should grasp before writing a contract, buying a house, or having a child. We were so prepared that we had ten pounds of legal treatises tucked in our bags, should we be asked a particularly complicated question about the palimony trials of Lee Marvin or Peter Frampton. Unfortunately for us, these subjects didn't come up nearly often enough. Most commonly, we were asked about our morality (or lack thereof), lifestyle, sexuality, religion, dish-washing habits, and how we introduced one another at a party, etc. More than once, sincerely outraged people accused us of contributing to the downfall of the moral and ethical standards of the nation. Although it was gratifying to our egos that anyone would think that we were that influential, it was a real shock to learn that, in the eyes of many, we were unpleasant panderers of immorality and depravity.

As we traveled from city to city, the airports and hotels changed, but the questions we were asked on the talk shows were remarkably similar. And when there were differences, they were almost always ones of phrasing, not content. For example, the detached and "very professional" type interviewer would ask, "Why do U.S. Census Bureau statistics show that so many people are living together these days as opposed to getting married?" while a feisty host would act like Mike Wallace or Barbara Walters and come right out with "Why don't you two get married if you really care for one another?" (try that one sometime at 7:30 a.m. in Detroit). And then there was the fatherly and concerned questioner, usually an ex-newsman with wonderful gray hair, a slightly lecherous twinkle in his eye and big white teeth, who would put his hand on Toni's knee and say, "My dear, now tell me honestly, isn't it true that way down in your heart of hearts, you would really like to be Mrs. Ralph Warner?" How did we respond to all of this? Not very well.

The truth was we were absolutely unprepared for what was happening to us. We had been close friends for eight years, business partners for six, and we had been living together for three years. Our relationship had evolved over the years with little thought to our legal status. This may sound a little strange, but remember our home was in Berkeley, California, a place where living together as part of a heterosexual couple was considered to be almost boringly straight. We hadn't gotten married, because, well, because we hadn't, that's all. Toni was a child of the sixties and never quite wanted to leave the Aquarian age, and Ralph, who is a few years older, had been married twice when he was in his twenties and had concluded that he wasn't very good at it.

How did we handle our predicament? Well, at first we tried to act lawyerly — that is, quickly mumbling a lot of complicated words that didn't mean much. But people are too media wise to be impressed by legal gobbledygook these days and we could feel the TV sets being switched off from Seattle to Scarsdale. In the end, we had to look right at each other and talk about the truth of our relationship. Surrounded as we were, by lights, cameras, a live studio audience and an ever-smiling host, this was no easy task. Gradually, however, a pleasant thing happened — we began to make sense to ourselves. If we hadn't become experts on the mental state that leads people to share a home without license or ceremony, at least we had something to say about our own relationship. And it was so simple that we had almost lost it under all the mock legal profundities and sociological doubletalk. We were living together because we loved each other a whole lot. Our relationship was based on chemistry, not common sense, and were we to get married the next day, probably very little would change.

This was still ducking the larger question of course. Chemistry may explain why people live and love together, but it doesn't explain why they do it without a marriage license. But ducking was really all we could do. We had developed some ideas as to why so many people are living together, but they were nothing we could explain in two and a half minutes between a deodorant commercial and a word on how to deal with constipation. Instead of trying, we decided to save them for this new edition of our book.

To understand why in the last quarter of the twentieth century millions of people's desire for both security and self-expression connected in a way that made living together — as opposed to marriage, communal living, living alone or living in a tree with an orangutan — seem like a sensible thing to do, it's helpful to review a little history. The past may not be of much help in charting the future, but by looking at our footprints, we can learn a great deal about how we got to where we are now.

Let's go back about one hundred years to the last quarter of the previous century. People like Chester Arthur and Grover Cleveland were in the White House, the steam engine and the steel rail were hot stuff, Victoria sat at the head of an empire upon which the sun never set, and the census of 1890 showed that the majority of Americans still lived on the farm. For our purposes, this last fact is most important. We often forget that, even though the industrial and technological juggernaut that would eventually pull almost everyone into urban areas had been a growing force for several centuries, most of our great-grandparents still followed a plow.

Rural America connects to our story because so many American values and ideals were formed there. The idea of "family" is one of the most important. This concept has taken very different forms in different cultures and circumstances but much of what we think about it today comes from the family farm. After all, the farm had been home for most Americans since European settlement.

In the nineteenth century, farm work was hard — one or two people couldn't do it efficiently — and farms were often lonely and isolated. Friends and neighbors and hired help were important, but when it came to getting the harvest in or even playing a little music on a winter night, they were no substitute for a large extended family. Or, put another way, it was the essence of peasant wisdom to raise pickers as well as corn. In rural America, an enduring marriage and a stable family made great sense — if you were going to be there to plant the crops, you had to be there to harvest them. And where was there to go anyway? Henry Ford was alive, but he hadn't yet invented the Tin Lizzie. Much was said about marriage and the sanctity of family being God's will — after all, this was the Victorian Age — but it is important to realize that when religious pieties were put aside, long-term marriage and big families were economic necessities. It is also worthy of note that life expectancies have greatly increased in the twentieth century so that getting married "until death do us part" is a lot longer commitment now than it used to be.

In 1890 the family commonly included Maiden Aunt Bess, slightly retarded Uncle Charley, Grandmother Elvira, and a home full of kids as well as several hired hands. But as the century turned and the Industrial Revolution hit high gear, things changed fast. The steady flow of people to the city became a flood. The economics of the family unit had changed. Food and space were not abundant in urban areas and suddenly Bess, Charley, Elvira and even all those kids were in the way.

"My, it costs a lot to raise kids these days, to say nothing of getting their teeth straightened and sending them to college," Papa said.

"You're right, dear, perhaps we only should have a couple," Mama replied.

And so it happened that, in a relatively few years, one style of living gave way to another and the family shrank like a wool blanket in a hot wash.

But a funny sort of "future shock" happened too. People seemed able to change their clothes and jobs and skills and educations and all the things necessary to keep up with the twentieth century a lot faster than they were able to adopt new ways of thinking about themselves and their relationships. Indeed, when faced with all the insecurities that Henry Ford, Alexander Bell, Tom Edison, Wilbur and Orville Wright and thousands of other pipers of the new age let loose, people seemed to reach back to find something "solid" on which to anchor their lives. Religion worked for some, and a sense of tradition for others, but for many Americans in the middle of the twentieth century, marriage and family seemed to be the important bricks when it came to building a sense of personal security. But sadly (and now we have begun to reach much of the immediate reason why so many have rejected marriage today) the family that many of our parents built their lives on was so truncated as to be almost nonexistent when compared to the extended family of rural America. It was a little as if our parents held tight to the myth of the family, but let the substance slip away. But myth or not, Americans pushed ahead with typical enthusiasm, wallpapering the countryside with "single family" houses — each one barely big enough for Mommy and Daddy, Billy, Sue and Spot.

For many people, suburban nuclear family life worked successfully. But for many others, it was an isolated, uncreative, stultifying existence with little opportunity for any sort of deviation from the norm. It was as if all the different personalities and eccentricities that had been a part of the extended family had been filtered out and everyone was expected to be "normal" and "fit in." Perhaps it's an understatement, but living in places such as Lafayette, Larkspur, Larchmont, La Mirada and Lincoln Park during the fifties and most of the sixties wasn't very sexy.

And then, of course, came the last half of the sixties — the years of reaction and rebellion when, with great love and great fun and great pain, the beliefs and value systems of the fifties were turned on their head. Sexual freedom, women's rights, acid and grass, looser work styles — yes, even crooked teeth — were in style and the Republicans were definitely out. But as you know if you experienced it, the crazy energy of the late sixties and early seventies was not the stuff of which lives are built. The barricades were fun for a while, but there wasn't much time for home cooking and a job well done. All the Woodstocks, women's marches, teach-ins, love-ins, and be-ins in the world didn't keep you warm on a rainy December night. So the new age learned an old lesson — freedom is the flip side of commitment and the space to be oneself must be measured against the ability to be intimate with others.

It was against this background in the middle seventies that living together became popular. For many it was a way to pull back a little from the revolution, without going all the way back to the fifties. It was a search for a workable small family in an age when, for most, it was unrealistic to go back to the extended family of the nineteenth century, and unpalatable to accept a concept of marriage that came with such a heavy load of failure, boredom and divorce. In short, it was a way to have a warm friend in the waterbed without signing up for life.

But then came Michele and Lee Marvin — those peculiarly unattractive people who dragged their pain and pride across our television screens every evening and shocked us out of the idea that living together was simple. My god, there it was — the naked, unpalatable truth — breaking up an unmarried relationship could be every bit as bad as getting a divorce. The fun was over, and like Farmer Brown catching Brer Rabbit in the cabbage patch, the lawyers had arrived. And right behind them came the media, with minicams and portable mikes, trying to get someone to explain what all the fuss was about. But television isn't very good at poetry and although they rolled miles of film, they missed the sense of optimism, joy and freedom that so many people who lived together experienced.

But what now? Have the muddy legalisms of the Marvin case, and the rest of the palimony suits, ruined the essence of living together, just as soaring divorce rates have done so much to tarnish the idea of marriage? Will the average couple conclude that since living together can involve as many legal complications as marriage, they may as well pick up a license? Or will people seek another solution such as living alone or living in unrelated groups? Our guess is that the lifestyles of the next generation will borrow some from all of these with no clear consensus that there is a "preferred" way to live. Almost certainly couples living together will make up a significant segment of society in the 1980's. Marriage isn't going to go away but it's unlikely to be again adopted by most couples until it becomes more open-ended. The idea that marriage is for life and that ending the relationship in divorce means that a couple has failed is another of those ideas that made great sense on the farm but one poisonous in our fast changing age.

But enough philosophy. Let's get on to what this book is really about — legal and practical information which will help unmarried couples cope creatively with the day-to-day problems of how their relationship intersects with the law.

# ex, Living Together, and The Law

## A. DEFINITIONS

ADULTERY—voluntary sexual intercourse between a married person and any person other than the lawful spouse. A single act is called an *adulterous act* or an *act of adultery*. When two persons are living together and at least one is married to someone else, this is called *adulterous cohabitation*.

BIGAMY

BIGAMY—the crime of marrying while one has a spouse still living, from whom no valid divorce has been effected. A *bigamist* is a person who commits bigamy. A *bigamous marriage* is a marriage contracted while at least one party was still married to another person.

CHASTE—virtuous. A married person, a widow or a divorcee could be described as chaste even though such person had previously enjoyed or, in the case of a married person, is still enjoying, sexual relations, as long as these relations occurred between persons lawfully married.

COHABITATION

COHABITATION—two persons of opposite sexes living together and having a sexual relationship without benefit of marriage. In a few states cohabitation has been defined as regular sex relations or even occasional sex relations, without living together, but this is unusual.

COMMON LAW MARRIAGE—a form of marriage valid in only a few states in which two persons of opposite sexes live together for a certain period of time with the intent of being married although they never have a marriage ceremony. In legal terms, this is called contracting a marriage.

COMMON LAW
MARRIAGE

COPULATION—sexual intercourse, coupling.

FELONY—a serious crime usually punishable by imprisonment for more than a year.

FINE—a sum of money that must be paid to a court by a person convicted of a crime.

FORNICATION—(1) voluntary sexual intercourse by an unmarried person with someone of the opposite sex; (2) adultery (biblical).

FINE

INCEST—sexual intercourse between persons so closely related that marriage between them is forbidden by law. Different states define incest differently, but all states legislate against marriage by children and their parents and grandparents, brothers and sisters (even if they are half brothers and sisters) and most, but not all states, include aunts, uncles and first cousins.

LEWD AND LASCIVIOUS—a term used in criminal statutes to describe sexual conduct, usually short of actual sexual intercourse; obscene; inciting to lust. For example, exposing oneself in a public place.

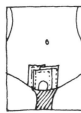

PROSTITUTION

MISDEMEANOR—a criminal offense less serious than a felony, usually punishable by a fine and/or a jail sentence of less than one year.

PROSTITUTION—the engaging in sexual relations for money.

SEDUCE—to induce a person to surrender his or her chastity. The act of seducing is called seduction.

SEDUCE

SODOMY—definition includes all the following: (1) "unnatural sexual intercourse"; (2) anal intercourse; (3) anal intercourse of a male with another male; (4) intercourse, anal or vaginal, of a person with an animal.

SPOUSE—either member of a married couple; one's husband or wife.

## B. IF IT FEELS GOOD, IT MAY BE ILLEGAL

It is illegal to have sex with a porcupine in Florida, to have unnatural sex in Arizona, to make love with someone you are not married to in Utah, and to live together (cohabit) in South Carolina. The maximum prison sentences for these heinous crimes vary from 6 months to 14 years. Pretty silly, huh?

Whether or not it is legal for you to live with and have sex with a person of the opposite (or same) sex if you are not married depends on where you live. It is legal in

Hawaii; it isn't in Alabama. Given the puritanical roots of this country, it is not surprising that we have had a hard time shaking off the sneaking suspicion that pleasure is tantamount to sin. In the past, if it felt good, it was probably illegal no matter where you lived. Although the nation's law books are still filled with an incredible array of sexual prohibitions, this is one area of the law that is undergoing a rapid change for the better. Whether it is a direct response to the "sexual revolution" or just a pragmatic realization that it is silly to make laws regulating the private areas of people's lives, the old sexual taboos are being dropped from the books. A good thing too as we were fast becoming a nation of criminals.

Most sex law reform is being accomplished by individual state legislatures decriminalizing private consensual acts between adults. This means doing away with crimes like cohabitation, adultery and oral copulation (see definitions).* This trend has been gathering momentum over the past decade and seems likely to continue. So far the following states have made all private sex acts between consenting adults, legal:**

| | |
|---|---|
| **Alaska** | **New Jersey** |
| **California** | **New Mexico** |
| **Colorado** | New York |
| **Connecticut** | **North Dakota** |
| **Delaware** | **Ohio** |
| **Hawaii** | **Oregon** |
| **Illinois** | Pennsylvania |
| **Indiana** | **South Dakota** |
| **Iowa** | **Vermont** |
| **Maine** | **Washington** |
| **Nebraska** | **West Virginia** |
| **New Hampshire** | Wisconsin |
| | **Wyoming** |

Because the law in this area is changing so fast, this list may not be completely up-to-date by the time you read this. If your state is still worried about how you fit your bodies together, check with your state legislator to find out if there are any current bills pending on decriminalization of consensual acts. A letter in support can't hurt. Obsolete laws are dangerous and unfair especially when you are the one violating them. While it is true that the comic book sex codes of most states are not rigorously enforced, every once in a while one of those old statutes falls off a shelf and hits somebody on the head. If it happens to be your head — you won't think it's very funny.

Another approach to wiping all sex laws off the books has been promoted by civil libertarians for years. Instead of approaching the problem one state at a time they have been trying to get a decision by the United States Supreme Court prohibiting all laws regulating the private consensual behavior among adults on the theory that such laws are an unconstitutional invasion of a citizen's right to privacy. The Supreme Court has yet to make this decision and many people feel that the present nine mostly elderly,

* The crime of adultery affects unmarried couples if one member of the couple is still married to someone else.
** In most states minors within a year or two of majority may live together with parental approval, but will face the strong possibility of action by juvenile authorities if parents are opposed.

18

mostly male justices are unlikely to do so. Like mountains, and almost as slowly it sometimes seems, Supreme Court Justices do change eventually, and there is hope that a future Court may be less rigid. Recently, the New Jersey courts have voided that state's fornication and sodomy laws on the grounds that they violated the right of privacy under both the state and federal constitutions.* In its landmark decision in *State v. Saunders* the New Jersey Supreme Court said: "We conclude that the conduct statutorily defined as fornication involves, buy its very nature, a fundamental personal choice. Thus, the statute infringes upon the right of privacy." Hopefully, the Supreme Court in other states that have not gone the legislative route of decriminalization will follow the New Jersey example.

You may be wondering how a fornication case came before the New Jersey Supreme Court in the first place. It happened like this. The defendant was originally charged with rape. He successfully defended his case on the theory that the alleged victim consented to the intercourse. He was acquitted. He was then charged and found guilty of fornication. We have found several other prosecutions for fornication or cohabitation in the last few years, but for the most part, the number of prosecutions for these kinds of "crimes" is low. If both of you are over 18, and neither is married to anyone else, you can practically speaking consider yourself safe from criminal prosecution for all private, common, heterosexual, sexual activities, no matter what your living arrangements. Local police departments and district attorneys have far better things to do with their time. Most sex laws are never used or are used only to harass gay people. Remember that we are not talking about violent sexual acts, sexual acts with children and prostitution and its associated activities, or sexual acts performed in public. Laws against these activities are enforced, and at least in the first two categories, should be. We are also not talking about bigamy (more than one marriage without a divorce) and incest (sex with relatives). They are punishable under the laws of all states, although bigamy, except in cases of fraud, is seldom prosecuted and incest is defined differently in different states.

Cohabitation, fornication and sodomy are still on the books as crimes in many states. These are the crimes that most affect people who are living together and so we include the following table indicating the states which still have statutes proscribing these acts:

---

* State v. Saunders, 381 A. 2d 333 (1977) and State v. Ciufinnni, 395 A. 2d 904 (1978).

# Sex Laws in the United States

| | OUTLAWS FORNICATION | OUTLAWS COHABITATION | OUTLAWS SODOMY AND/OR ORAL COPULATION BETWEEN CONSENTING ADULTS |
|---|---|---|---|
| Alabama | No | No | Yes |
| Arizona | No | Yes | Yes |
| Arkansas | No | No | Yes |
| Florida | No | Yes | Yes |
| Georgia* | Yes | No | Yes |
| Idaho | Yes | Yes | Yes |
| Kansas** | No | No | Yes |
| Kentucky | No | No | Yes |
| Louisiana | No | No | Yes |
| Maryland | No | No | Yes |
| Massachusetts*** | Yes | Yes | Yes |
| Michigan | No | Yes | Yes |
| Minnesota | No | No | Yes |
| Mississippi | Yes | Yes | Yes |
| Missouri | No | No | Yes |
| Montana | No | No | Yes |
| Nevada | No | No | Yes |
| North Carolina | Yes | Yes | Yes |
| Oklahoma | No | No | Yes |
| Rhode Island | Yes | Yes | Yes |
| South Carolina | Yes | Yes | Yes |
| Tennessee | No | No | Yes |
| Texas** | No | No | Yes |
| Utah* | Yes | No | Yes |
| Virginia | Yes | Yes | Yes |
| Washington, D. C. | Yes | Yes | Yes |

* In Georgia and Utah, there's no separate statute for cohabitation, but it is probably illegal under the fornication statute.

** In Kansas and Texas, the sodomy laws only prohibit homosexual conduct. Kansas' sodomy statute specifically exempts consenting adults of opposite sexes, and Texas' law specifically outlaws homosexual conduct.

*** A Massachusetts appeals court has noted that the "crimes of fornication...and...cohabitation are never, or substantially never made the subject of enforcement." *Fort v. Fort,* (1981) 425 N.E. 2d 754. This may be some authority for not enforcing these laws in the future.

If you would like to find out more information about laws (and penalties for violators) regulating fornication, cohabitation, sodomy, oral copulation and assorted unnatural acts in your state, go to your local law library and look in the penal code under the index headings you are interested in.

## C. COMMON LAW MARRIAGE

There is a widespread belief among many that if you live with a person for a certain period of months or years, you are automatically married. In the great majority of states, including California and New York, this is simply not true. A few states still recognize what are called "common law marriages". A state that recognizes such marriages requires that both persons **intend** to enter into a common law marriage; the length of time you live together is not in itself important, but may be considered insofar as it tends to show intent. Thus merely living together doesn't create a common law marriage even in those states where it is recognized. And, if one or both parties are married to someone else, no amount of intent and living together can create a valid common law marriage.

There is one little trick in this area, however. A state that does not provide for common law marriage within its own boundaries will recognize such a marriage which was properly formed in a state that does recognize it. For example, Colorado recognizes common law marriages while California does not. Therefore, if Bob and Carol started living together in Los Angeles in 1947 and are still living together and have never moved from the state of California, they are not legally married, even if both parties thought they were.* However, if Ted and Alice started living together in Colorado in 1975 with the intention of forming a common law marriage and have been living together since that time, both Colorado and California will recognize the marriage as valid.

The following chart indicates the laws of the different states regarding common law marriage. If you have any questions regarding the status of your relationship, you would be wise to do some research as to the law in your own state. Frequently the question of whether there was sufficient "intent" to form a marriage is tricky. There are no specific laws as to what conduct shows "intent to be married". Intent, or lack of it, is normally found from the facts of each situation. Such things as using the same last name, filing joint income tax returns, and holding yourselves out to the community to be married, etc. would be important. If you want to protect what you consider a marriage, or prevent yourself from being married against your wishes, it is better to do this now than to wait until you break up. If you do decide to split, a common law marriage must be ended by divorce, just like a marriage with a ceremony, and you cannot legally marry another person until that common law marriage has been terminated by legal proceedings or death.

---

* Many states that do not recognize common law marriage give certain property rights to people who are living in situations similar to marriage or who falsely believe that they are married. Often a person living in this kind of situation is called a "putative spouse". See Chapter 7.

```
STATES RECOGNIZING COMMON LAW MARRIAGE

Alabama                Iowa              Oklahoma
Colorado               Kansas            Pennsylvania
Columbia, District of  Montana           Rhode Island
Georgia                Ohio              South Carolina
Idaho                                    Texas


STATES NOT RECOGNIZING COMMON LAW MARRIAGE

Alaska         Maine            New York
Arizona        Maryland         North Carolina
Arkansas       Massachusetts    North Dakota
California      Michigan         Oregon
Connecticut    Minnesota        South Dakota
Delaware       Mississippi      Tennessee
Florida        Missouri         Utah
Hawaii         Nebraska         Vermont
Illinois       Nevada           Virgin Islands
Indiana        New Hampshire*   Washington
Kentucky       New Jersey       West Virginia
Louisiana      New Mexico       Wisconsin
                                Wyoming


* However, living together in New Hampshire for at least three years until one
partner dies results in a valid marriage for inheritance purposes.
```

**NOTE:** If you live together in a state recognizing common law marriages and do not wish to be married, it is a particularly good idea to sign a statement making it clear you do not intend to be married. If you use the same last names and/or mix property together it is essential that you do this. Here is a sample agreement which you may want to use separately or integrate into one of the contracts in Chapter 4.

## SAMPLE AGREEMENT

Wanda Walters and Walter Walters agree as follows:

1. That they have been and plan to continue to live together as two free independent beings and that neither has ever intended to enter into any form of marriage, common law or otherwise.

_____          _____
Date                                 Wanda Walters


_____          _____
Date                                 Walter Walters
                    (Notarization is optional)

# ractical Aspects of Living Together

===

## A. GETTING TOGETHER

When people come together to walk the same path for awhile, they bring not only themselves and their love for one another, but tend also to drag along all sorts of objects, debts, animals, relationships, etc. We will let you work out your own problems involving the goldfish, Great Danes, and former mothers-in-law, but will give you a quick rundown of your rights in more mundane areas:

### 1. Debts

By living with someone you take absolutely no responsibility for their debts. Your wages cannot be attached and your property cannot be threatened to pay for your friend's overdue bills. If your friend's creditors contact you, a good chuckle should handle the problem. Should your friend declare bankruptcy, your property will not be taken, **as long as you have kept it separate.**

**WARNING:** If your friend is having debt problems, be very careful not to mix property together in a joint bank account, in joint ownership of a car, or in any other way. Do not enter into an agreement to share and pool earnings and accumulations. In this situation it would be advisable to sign a contract keeping everything separate (such as Contract I in the Appendix) so that there can be no possible confusion as far as your friend's creditors are concerned. Because, if your property does become commingled (say in a joint bank account) with that of your friend, you will, at the very least, have problems explaining to your friend's greedy creditors that some of it is yours and you may end up losing out in the confusion.

## 2. Property Acquired Before Getting Together

Each person retains complete ownership of all possessions owned prior to getting together. We include as part of the contracts set out in the Appendix a page where the separate property of each party can be listed (see Chapter 4). One person can, of course, give the other objects of his (her) property, or a part interest in a particular piece of property. If a major item is given, a little note setting forth the facts would be helpful. We have seen a lot of problems where people disagree as to what was or was not a gift.

## 3. Property Acquired After Getting Together

Generally, it is our opinion that the easiest and cleanest way to handle your economic affairs is to keep them separate. As we noted above, it is imperative to do this if one of you is having debt problems. But even when this is not the case, a lot of potential complications can be avoided by each of you maintaining your financial independence and keeping your property and debts separate. If you keep three simple plans in mind, you will have a smoother relationship with fewer bitter feelings at the end. These plans are:

❍ Enter into an agreement keeping your earnings and accumulations separate as in Contract I in the Appendix (see Chapter 4).

❍ Do not have joint accounts or make joint purchases unless absolutely necessary. Do not mix money or business affairs together except in emergencies. Always keep your own bank account and do not add extra signatures to your charge accounts. Continue to use your own names and do not pass yourself off as husband and wife. Do not cosign loans or credit agreements unless you are completely willing to assume all payment obligations if your friend cannot or will not pay.

❍ If you do purchase expensive items that you intend to belong to both of you, write out an agreement that sets out your understanding. This should include how the items are being paid for, what will happen to them if you break up and what will happen if one of you dies (see Chapter 4, Section B for sample joint purchase agreements). Be sure that each of you signs the agreement and that a copy is attached to your over-all, keep-things-separate contract. If you buy a house together, you will need a more formal document as outlined in Chapter 6. If you jointly purchase an automobile, there are certain additional registration procedures to follow (see Section F below).

If you each have adequate income and each of you pays your share of the expenses, the above plans should be simple to follow. However, if you have a relationship where one of you works and supports the other, it is just as important that you have written understandings, although they may be a bit more complex (see Chapter 4). This is especially true if one of you works and the other has free access to the money and makes purchases and pays bills. At the end of such a relationship, there should never be the need for one person to say, "I supported him (or her) for ten years; he (or she) did not contribute anything and now the lazy bum has gone off and left me." Or, conversely, "I gave up my career to cook and clean for him (or her) for ten years, and he (she) said he'd (she'd) support me forever and here I am left alone with no support." Whatever your financial understanding, it should be absolutely clear that each person is free and equal in the living arrangement, whether he happens to bring home the bacon, or cooks it and cleans up the mess afterward.

Remember, you entered the relationship freely. Each of you has the right to leave it freely. If you feel you are being taken advantage of, examine your own head and the situation. If you are unhappy, perhaps it is time to dissolve the living arrangement.

## 4. Names

Normally, each member of an unmarried couple keeps their own last name. This is easy, legal and creates few if any practical problems. However, occasionally an unmarried couple will want to use the same last name. This, too, can be done with little difficulty as it is legal for a person to change their last name in any way they wish unless by doing it they invade someone else's privacy or attempt to defraud someone such as a creditor.

A name can be changed by simply using the new name consistently (the usage method) or by petitioning a court and getting a court order (the court petition method).* The usage method has the obvious advantage of avoiding going to court, but without an official paper it can take years to convince all the private and government agencies that register you to accept your new name (getting a passport in your new name is a particular hassle). On the other hand, the court petition method involves an initial bit of trouble, but once you get your court order, everyone will accept your new name pronto.

**NOTE:** If you live in a state recognizing common law marriage and both use the same last name, some implication may be created that you intend to be married. Assuming you don't, sign a brief agreement like the one in Chapter 1. It is also possible that using the same last name, considered along with other factors, might lead a court to conclude you intended to share your earnings and accumulations under an implied living together contract (see Chapter 4). Therefore, if you wish to keep your money and property separate, but share your last name, you should be sure to sign one of the agreements in Chapter 4 which will make your intention clear.

---

*How to Change Your Name (California Edition), Loeb & Brown, Nolo Press, gives complete forms and instructions for both types of name change in California.

## B. SHARING BANK ACCOUNTS

Our advice to anyone considering sharing a bank account, either checking or savings, is: DON'T. If each person has his (her) own account and pays the agreed-upon expenses, there is no possibility of confusion. Canceled checks serve as receipts. Our experience has been that joint accounts often lead to confusion, paranoia and bitterness. Of course, we are definitely prejudiced in this matter. We give the same advice to married couples.

There are no legal problems associated with opening joint accounts. Banks will be happy to take care of your money under any name or names. If you insist on having joint accounts, the bank will assist you in deciding how many signatures will be necessary to write a check or make a withdrawal from a savings account. You may decide that either one of you should be able to get money by signing for it, or you may decide that it is necessary for both of you to sign. Remember, if you do have a joint account, you are both responsible for all checks drawn on the account even if the other person takes all the money and disappears. Further, if your partner takes all the money out of the savings account and leaves, the bank is not responsible unless two signatures were required for withdrawal.

## C. CHARGE ACCOUNTS AND BUYING ON TIME

You and your friend may want to buy on credit or establish joint charge accounts. Again, if you were to ask us if this is a good idea, we would say NO. If you are both working, there is no reason why you cannot each have your own account. This means that you each deal with your creditors on your own terms, and you do not have to worry about the purchases of the other party. However, in spite of this practical advice some people are determined to share "everything" with their partners. The following sections are included on the theory that if we can't talk you out of it, we may as well give you a hand.

This is also a good place to tell you that the best one-word definition we know for most cosigners is: "IDIOT". A cosigner is a person who by signing his name fully obligates himself to pay another person's debt if that person fails to do so, whatever the reason. The cosigner gets none of the benefits of the transaction (often a loan) and often all of the burdens. Should the primary debtor default, the cosigner can be sued if he or she doesn't pay voluntarily, and is subject to wage garnishments if he or she doesn't pay the judgment. A person should cosign only if he or she is fully prepared to pay the debt if the debtor defaults.

## D. HOW TO APPLY FOR CREDIT

There are still some stores that will not set up joint accounts for unmarried couples. Although this is a somewhat murky legal area, it is the opinion of staff members of the Federal Trade Commission that such a denial would be a violation of the Equal Credit Opportunity Act (see Section E). However, after conferring with representatives of a number of national retail chains, we have found that credit discrimination against the unmarried couple is mostly a thing of the past. Most of the major stores will open joint credit accounts for unmarried couples if they have joint accounts at all.* After all, it is to their advantage to have as many persons as possible responsible for a debt. If you should run into a situation where joint accounts are limited to married couples, do not pretend to be married to qualify. A little misstatement now can cause big problems later, especially if you ever have to file for bankruptcy. In this case your creditor could claim you obtained credit by fraud and prevent you from getting rid of the debt.

When you are dealing with a store that is happy to issue you a joint charge account, remember that you are both legally responsible for all charges made on the account by either of you, or by the person that has the consent of one of you to make charges. This means that if Keija allows her cousin Floyd to use the joint charge card that she has with Felix and Floyd runs up a bill for $1,000, Keija **and** Felix are both responsible for the debt even if Felix opposed or did not know about Floyd's use of the card. Also, if Felix leaves Keija and uses the charge card on a spending spree across the country, both Felix **and** Keija are legally responsible for all charges made by Felix.

If, in spite of our warnings, you and your partner do open joint credit accounts, we suggest that you arrange the account so that both of your signatures are required in order to charge. In addition to guaranteeing that the card is not abused, this may serve as a brake on impulse buying.

**WARNING:** As we will see in Chapter 3, in some states contracts between unmarried couples can be oral or sometimes even implied from the circumstances of a relationship if there is no written agreement. The sharing of charge accounts might well be one factor a court would take into consideration in deciding whether a couple had established a contract to share earnings and other property in some states.

**IMPORTANT:** If the two of you do break up, be sure to inform all your joint creditors that you wish to close out your account immediately. We have seen many cases where friends forgot to do this and ended up paying for an ex-lover's purchases. It is not a good idea to simply divide the accounts and agree one person can use some of the accounts while the other person uses the others. Remember, you are still liable for all purchases if your name is still on the account, even if your relationship is over.

### E. CREDIT AND CREDIT AGENCIES

A store or a lending institution need not lend to any particular person. Of course, stores normally lend to people they consider good financial risks and refuse to lend to poor financial risks. However, no one seems to agree on just what a "poor financial risk" is, and what factors contribute to determining the financial responsibility of an

---

* Montgomery Wards and some other large stores handle the problem by not issuing joint accounts to anyone. Obviously, if they don't issue joint accounts to married couples, they can't be thought of as discriminating if they don't issue them to the unmarried. Almost all stores, including Wards, do allow a cardholder to authorize additional signatures on his or her account. This works the same as a joint account for some, but by no means all purposes. For example, only the person whose name is on the account is legally liable to pay the store.

applicant for credit. If a person has no apparent source of income, he is not a good risk. If a person has a history of being unemployed for long periods of time, he is not a good risk. If a person has immediate plans to leave the country, he is not a good risk. If a person has a low income and a lot of dependents or a lot of expenses, it is reasonable to assume that he is not a good risk. But what about factors that are seemingly unrelated to income or ability to pay?

Congress has passed laws which say that creditors cannot discriminate against certain groups or classes of people. It is unlawful for creditors to discriminate on the basis of "race, color, religion, national origin, sex, marital status, or age, or because all or part of a person's income derives from any public assistance program."* Some creditors apparently claim that "marital status" only refers to whether you are married or single and does not prevent them from discriminating against unmarried couples. This is now illegal.**

This sounds pretty good, especially since the law also says that a creditor who fails to comply with this law may have to pay an individual who has been discriminated against $10,000 plus any money that individual actually lost as a result of the discrimination. (If a large group of people wins a suit against the creditor for unlawful discrimination, the creditor may have to pay up to $500,000 for violating the law.) But, and this is the big "but" that always seems to be present when we try to solve human problems by legislation, the law becomes very complicated as it attempts to define "discrimination". For example, an inquiry into a person's marital status is not discrimination if "such inquiry is for the purpose of ascertaining the creditor's rights and remedies applicable to a particular extension of credit, and not to discriminate in a determination of creditworthiness." This sounds like a pretty fine line to us. Also, state property laws may be considered by a creditor in deciding whether to extend credit. This means that a creditor's decision in one state may be OK while it would violate the law in another state.

* This is called the "Equal Credit Opportunity Act," 15 U.S. 1691.
** In a federal court case on the D.C. Circuit, the court ruled that if a couple was going to be jointly liable on a joint debt, unmarried status is no excuse for refusing to aggregate incomes and that all marital status discrimination is banned by the Act. *Markham v. Colonial Mortgage Services Co.* (1979) 605 F 2d 566. A California appeals court said substantially the same thing in regard to rental housing; if the income of a married couple would be aggregated to see if they had sufficient income, so should the income of an unmarried couple. *Hess v. Fair Employment & Housing Commission* 187 Cal. Rptr. 712.

The regulations issued to the Federal Reserve System say specifically that a creditor cannot require use of a married name, but must allow credit to be issued in either your birth-given name or a combined surname. The regulations also say you can be required to reveal alimony and child support payments that you are required to make, but not payments you receive, unless you are relying on them to establish your income for credit purposes. A creditor may not completely ignore your income from child support or alimony payments in determining your creditworthiness, but may consider how likely they are to be paid. A creditor may not completely ignore income from a part-time job. A creditor may not ask you questions about your birth control practices, or whether you intend to have children. A creditor cannot terminate your account or require a re-application if you change your name or marital status unless there is evidence you are unwilling or unable to pay your bill. Also, if the creditor denies you credit, he must inform you of the reason for the denial.

There haven't been many cases testing the effect of the Equal Credit Opportunity Act. However, under this law, it has become much easier for married women to buy on credit without having their husbands involved in the credit transaction. It is also easier for unmarried couples to open accounts either joint or separate. If you feel you were discriminated against, contact the nearest regional office of the Federal Trade Commission (for non-bank related credit problems) or the Federal Reserve Board (for bank-related credit problems). If you feel that yours is a clear case of discrimination, you may wish to contact an attorney (you could inquire through women's organizations or the ACLU) to bring a lawsuit on your behalf.

**REMEMBER:** Being refused credit is often a cloud with a silver lining, since what is credit really other than a license to buy lots of things you can probably do without at prices that exceed their true worth to you while paying unreasonable amounts of interest for the privilege?

Some organizations specialize in keeping credit files on individuals. Normally, these "credit bureaus" are part of, or have close working relationships with, bill collection agencies. Creditors and other sources contribute information to these files and prospective creditors can then contact the agency and obtain the information contained in your file for a small fee. Some of these agencies claim that they keep information only as to past performance in paying debts, but this is not true. All sorts of personal information, completely unrelated to financial matters routinely appears in these files.* Some of these agencies also claim that they do not cross-index unmarried persons living together (husbands and wives are always filed together) but this may not be true. In some cases, a bad credit rating on the person with whom you are living will also show up on your credit rating and may prevent your obtaining of credit. Your file will contain every name you have been known by and, if Keija has applied for credit as "Mrs. Felix Finnegan", Felix may find the bills listed under his name even if he did not sign for the account. This is especially true if the couple has consistently represented itself to creditors as "Mr. and Mrs. Felix Finnegan".

---

* For a good rundown on credit bureaus and collection agencies and a thorough discussion of your rights, see *The California Debtors' Handbook – Billpayers' Rights,* Honigsberg and Warner — coupon side back cover.

**IMPORTANT:** Under the Federal Fair Credit Reporting Act you have the right to go to a credit bureau (there may be more than one in your area) to find out what is in your file. If false information is in the file, you have the right to get it corrected and may also put information in the file to explain your point of view, where you believe a wrong impression is being made.

If you do decide to open a joint account, be aware that not only **your** "sins" but also the "sins" of your partner may haunt you for a long time. If your friend takes off, leaving a large debt behind that you pay despite the fact that you are not legally obligated to do so, your slow payment record will still remain in your file. Again, do not represent yourself as married if you are not. Give only correct information on your application. Credit is not worth the problems that can follow from this kind of deception.

## F. BUYING A MOTOR VEHICLE

Occasionally, a couple may decide to jointly purchase a motor vehicle. If only one of you has signed the loan from the lending institution but both of you are contributing funds toward its purchase, an agreement should be prepared like the one found in Chapter 4, Section B. When the vehicle is registered with the state, you may register it any way you choose. If your intention is that the vehicle belongs to both of you, you should register it in both your names. If your intention is that the vehicle belongs to one of you, then register the car only in the name of that person. Again, the important point is that you agree **before** you make the purchase as to who shall own and use the item and who shall pay for it. In most states there are three types of joint ownership of motor vehicles:

1. Vehicle registered in the form "Felix Finnegan **or** Keija Adams". If this form of registration is used, then if one person dies the ownership certification and registration card can be reassigned to the surviving joint tenant by the Department of Motor Vehicles without the necessity of going through a probate proceeding. **However**, this type of joint ownership allows either party to sell the vehicle at any time without the knowledge or consent of the other joint tenant.

2. Motor vehicle registered in the form "Felix Finnegan **and** Keija Adams". If this form of registration is used, the signatures of both parties are required to transfer the title of the vehicle. However, if one party dies, the other party may have to go through probate proceedings in order to obtain title to the vehicle. We say "may" because some states such as California exempt estates from probate when they are small. If you use this form of ownership, a will is necessary to pass your share of the property to your friend if you die (see Chapter 11).

3. Motor vehicles registered in the form "Felix Finnegan **and** Keija Adams, JTRS" (Joint Tenancy with Right of Survivorship). If registration is in this form, both signatures are required to transfer title to the vehicle, but, at the death of one party, the survivor may obtain title to the vehicle from the Department of Motor Vehicles without going through probate proceedings.

**NOTE:** Before relying on this information, check with the government agency in charge of registration for your state. They should be able to advise you about the different methods available.

## G. TRAVEL

Looking over the next hill, just across an ocean, or perhaps for the end of a rainbow seems to be one of our great national joys (some would say diseases). How you will travel, whether strapped into a great silver bird or wandering slowly down a country road, is less important than the fact that almost certainly, you will travel. When you move about together, you are bound to experience those funny (sometimes scary) moments when, with pen poised in hand over hotel or motel register, you freeze — absolutely don't know what to write. You probably don't want to break laws unnecessarily, but you also don't want to be hassled, especially don't want the poetry of your trip ripped off.

But how to register? In some places only one name is necessary. The number of persons that will be occupying the room must be stated, but only one signature is required. It is sensible to start by registering in this way and to let the motel employee ask for more specifics if he or she wants them. Where both persons must sign or be identified, the question arises as to whether you register as "Keija and Felix Finnegan" or "Felix Finnegan and Keija Adams". Many places prefer that you register under the first alternative. They may not care if you are married or not, but they like to have the appearance of caring. Some places may hassle you if you register under the second method, and, if the issue is forced, refuse to give you lodging. However, we have found in recent years that greed has triumphed over conventional "morality". The sheer volume of business due to unmarried couples traveling is an economically persuasive argument to stop hassling. As part of doing this book we talked to a number of national and international hotel chains including Hilton and Hyatt and found that they have adopted an official policy of "not inquiring" into the status of a couple, even if they register using separate last names.

Sometimes travel discount rates are available only to married couples. It is more common these days that they are extended to any two adults traveling together, but you may still run into a chance to save money by saying that you are married. Do you run any legal risk by doing this? No. For purposes of tours, tickets, etc. you are safe enough claiming the status that will get you the cheapest rates. As lots of married couples use different last names these days, no one is likely to hassle you.

**WARNING:** But what happens if a hotel or motel does discriminate against you because of your marital status? Do you have any legal recourse? Absent a local ordinance, which exist in a number of major cities and some university towns, the answer is usually NO.

## H. DISCRIMINATION IN EMPLOYMENT

Many private employers will not be aware of your living situation unless you are in an extremely important or sensitive position. If you are unlucky enough to have an employer who threatens your job when he discovers you are living in an unmarried state, you may wish to consult an attorney about whether or not you can do anything to protect yourself. In most cases, the attorney will probably advise you that there is little that can be done. Traditionally, private employers are not required to hire or retain particular employees. They are free to terminate employment just as an employee is free to resign and move on. Recently, however, many national corporations have announced policies of not discriminating on the basis of marital status. If such a policy has been announced by your employer, you have a legal right to rely on it.

However, the situation is somewhat different for employment in state, county and city jobs. Police departments, school boards, post offices are all subject to the principles found in the Fourteenth Amendment of the Constitution. Unfortunately, a U.S. Supreme Court decision in this area is a horrible one in which the court, over Justice Marshall's eloquent dissent, refused to consider the case of Rebecca Hollenbaugh and Fred Philburn, who were fired from their employment at the Carnegie Free Library in Connesville, Pa., for living together.* The lower federal courts held that, while there needed to be some relationship between the reason for the firing and the performance on the job, that this test was met because the couple was living in a state of "open adultery." However, in a much wiser decision, the more enlightened California Supreme Court has ruled that gay employees of private public utilities can't be fired for living together.**

Court decisions protecting unmarried couples have traditionally been strongest in the area of federal employment. In 1967 a postal clerk in California was dismissed from his job because his living with a women he was not married to constituted "immoral conduct". He appealed and the Federal District Court of Northern California decided that his dismissal was unconstitutional becasue the post office had failed to show that his private sex life had any connection with the responsibilities of his position so that his firing was arbitrary and a denial of due process. Also, the post office had failed to show a "compelling reason" to justify the invasion of his Ninth Amendment right to privacy. Other court decisions have gone on to clearly establish that the private living arrangements of public employees is not normally relevant to their jobs.

---

* 99 X. Ct. 734 (1978).

** In the case of *Gay Law Students Association v. Pacific Telephone and Telegraph*, (1979) 156 Cal. Rptr. 14. In another move toward sanity, the Virginia Supreme Court recently upheld the right of a woman to become an attorney even though she had a live-in lover. *Cord v. Gibb*, 254 S.E. 2d 71 (1979).

## I. PAYING YOUR TAXES

### 1. Comparing Tax Rates for Married and Unmarried Couples

The American tax system is incredibly complicated and not always logical. Many ordinary people are so confused and intimidated by tax forms and regulations that they hire an agency or "expert" to prepare their returns. Part of the confusion arises in classifying income, taking deductions, and claiming exemptions or credits. Part of it arises from the fact that different people pay different *rates* of income tax, depending on their marital or family status.

An unmarried person may file as a single person or, in certain cases, qualify as an "unmarried head of household." In some cases, a person recently widowed may file as married filing jointly. A married person may file either a joint return, or a married person's separate return. In some cases, a married person who is separated may qualify to file an unmarried person's return. What difference does it make how one files? Quite a bit, since the tax rate varies widely by method of filing.

For instance, Susan has a $15,000 income. For the 1983 tax year (tax due April 15, 1984), on the short form 1040A, she pays $2097 if single, $2000 if an unmarried head of household, $2532 if married and filing separately, and $1676 if married filing jointly and her spouse has no income. Of course, one can't file any way one wants. The filing must, with certain exceptions, correspond to the actual family status.

In the above example, a married joint return filer paid the lowest rate of tax. Is it always better, tax-wise, to be married? NO. In many situations, living together couples will pay a lower rate of tax than married couples.

Consider the following example. Felix and Keija live together. They **both** work, and they **each** earn $20,000. They file the short form 1040A and do not itemize deductions. Each will pay taxes on $20,000 of income, which at 1983 single rates is $3369 each, or $6738 altogether. Were they married (filing jointly), they would pay tax on their joint income of $40,000. Since it is a higher income, they would pay a higher rate. Although they could deduct $2000 from their income for being married,* they still pay $7604, which is $866 more than if they file separately as single persons.

In another example, let's say Felix makes $35,000 and Keija $40,000. Since they live together, he would pay $8313 and she would pay $10,313, which is $18,626 altogether. Were they married, they would pay $21,294.** They save $2668 by remaining unmarried. However, if Felix was making $60,000 and Keija $10,000, if they stayed single, he would pay $19,473 in tax and she would pay $1021, totaling $20,494. If they were married, taking into account their marriage deduction, they would pay $19,974, so being married would save them $520.

Of course, all this is going to vary greatly with the individual or couple, especially as we have not taken dependents or other variable factors into account. Working couples with fairly-similar incomes will probably find some tax advantage in

---

* Married working couples are entitled to a deduction to partially alleviate what was called the "marriage tax penalty" which used to result in middle income married working couples paying much more tax than a similar couple living together. The deduction (under Tax Code section 221) is 10% of the income of the lower earnings spouse, to a maximum deduction of $3000. This credit has narrowed the gap between living together and married couples, but if both work, there is still usually an advantage to living together.
** This takes into account the marriage tax penalty relief deduction.

living together. Couples that have only one income, or widely disparate incomes where one partner has a very low income and the other a middle or high income, will probably find some tax advantage in being married, which will increase if the lower earning person has dependents. We don't recommend you make your marriage-or-living together decision solely on the basis of tax tables. After all, the tax rates shift from year to year (and so, probably, will your income).

We have been asked if it's legal to divorce and continue to live together to qualify for lower tax rates? The answer is, yes, as long as you don't marry and divorce every year or so to try to get the benefits of both marriage and living together. If you do this, the IRS will take the position that your divorce is a sham and prosecute you for tax avoidance.

## 2. Dependents and Taxes

May you claim your roommates or their children as your dependents, even if they are not related to you? Internal Revenue Code 152 defines dependents as close relatives or unrelated persons who live in the taxpayer's household as principal place of abode and are supported by the taxpayer. However, the IRS Regulations say that "an individual is *not* a member of taxpayer's household if at any time during the taxable year the relationship between such individual and taxpayer is in violation of local law." IRS Regs. 1.151-1-(b).

A federal court interpreted this to say that a North Carolina man could not claim the woman he was living with as his dependent since cohabitation is illegal in North Carolina.* In states where living together is legal, you can file a dependency deduction as long as you meet the rest of the requirements; i.e., your roommate and his or her children have their "principal abode" in your household, you provide more than one half their support, they have not earned more than $1,000 each,** they have not filed a joint return with anyone else, and they meet certain residency requirements. For details see the Internal Revenue Service Guidelines.

---

* *Ensminger v. Commissioner of Internal Revenue* (1979) 610 F2d 189.
** After 1985, this changes to the "exemptive amount."

## J. WELFARE, FOOD STAMPS, MEDI-CARE

Welfare regulations are much like quicksand. What looks safe, solid and reliable one minute can gobble you up the next. Changing rules seem to be part of a system that has never found a comfortable place in the American consciousness. So before you rely on what we say here, check with your local social services agency.

If a person (usually a woman) receiving welfare under the Aid For Dependent Children (AFDC) Program starts living with a man, can she continue to receive her monthly check? Yes, as long as the man is not actually contributing to her support or the support of the children, welfare will not be cut off or reduced.*Some welfare departments will require considerable proof that money is being kept separate, others are not so tight. The welfare department is not supposed to be interested in the physical relationship between the mother and the man, only in what he contributes. It is always wise to call and find out exactly what local procedures are so that you can adjust your situation to fit any technicalities.

Both the AFDC mother and the unrelated male will have to sign a welfare department statement stating under penalty of perjury the amount of money, if any, he pays. Most welfare departments have a requirement that a man who has income contribute at least the fair cost of his monthly expenses to the family unit. In many states this is assumed to be about $120. A man who does this should be sure that his contributions are kept separate and are only used for his own expenses. He has no legal duty to contribute to the support of either the AFDC mother or her children, and the welfare department cannot legally force him to do so. If they do subtract money from the mother's grant because he is living in the house, an appeal should be taken (called a fair hearing). To do this, see your nearest legal aid or welfare rights group for help.

**HINT:** Find out what the minimum monthly contribution for a male for his own expenses is in your state. Document that the man pays this much and no more and does not contribute to the expenses of the woman or her children. This will result in the AFDC mother keeping most or all of her grant. If you report that the man pays more than the minimum, you will lose welfare benefits.

**EXAMPLE:** Tara and her two children are receiving a monthly grant under the AFDC Program. Ben, who makes $1,000 per month, moves in and contributes $120 per month for his rent and household expenses (Tara has checked to see that this is the minimum in her state). Tara can keep the majority of her grant as long as Ben doesn't provide additional money for her support or for the support of the children. Tara should keep detailed records as to income and expenditures to prove that she is independent. As long as the records are neat and seem sensible, the welfare department is unlikely to demand proof for every item.

Rules on food stamps are a little tighter. If Tara is living with Ben, it will be assumed that they are eating together. Since Ben has a substantial income, food

---

* This assumes that the man is not the father of the woman's child(ren). If parents live together with their child it will be assumed that they are a family unit.

stamps will be cut off. However, if Tara can prove that she buys and stores her food separately and doesn't share with Ben, she can also keep her food stamps.

**HINT:** The amount of money received under your AFDC check is quite large in comparison to the value of the food stamps. You may be wise not to be "too greedy" and press for food stamps too. If you do, you risk the authorities taking a closer look at your situation — something many people on welfare find that it is wiser not to encourage.

Medical benefits are figured the same way AFDC benefits are. This means that you can live with someone and keep the medical card for you and your children as long as the person who you are living with doesn't contribute to your support.

## K. SOCIAL SECURITY

The Social Security Program discriminates against unmarried couples. If you are married to a wage earner covered by Social Security, you are eligible to receive retirement benefits. If you are the widow, widower or divorced spouse of a wage earner, you can also get benefits.* However, there are no benefits for people who have been living together unless, of course, they have been individually earned by each wage earner.** Is this unfair? Of course it is, but it is nevertheless the law. If the trend away from marriage continues, changes may be made, but as of now a non-wage earner will come out ahead financially if married to a wage earner rather than living with the same person.

**COMMON LAW MARRIAGE NOTE:** If you have been living with someone covered by Social Security in a state which recognizes common law marriage (see Chapter 2) and your friend has died or become disabled, you may be able to claim that you were, in fact, married and thus qualify for benefits. Common law marriage is just as valid as formal marriage for Social Security purposes.

If you are a divorced wife, 62 years of age or older, you can get benefits on your ex-spouse's Social Security records if he is getting payments and your marriage lasted at least ten years (instead of 20 years). If you are a surviving divorced spouse, survivor's benefits can now start as early as age 60 (50 if you are disabled).

---

* If you have questions concerning what you are or will be entitled to, call Social Security and ask for a pamphlet entitled "Your Social Security." For more details see the *Sourcebook for Older Americans: Income, Rights & Benefits*, Nolo Press.
** Children of deceased or disabled members of unmarried couples are eligible for benefits if paternity can be proven. See Chapter 8, Section I.

## L. INSURANCE

Generally speaking, it's now possible for unmarried couples to purchase most types of insurance at competitive rates. However, it's still possible to encounter discrimination in some circumstances:

### 1. Unmarried Couples and Life Insurance

Life insurance used to be a particular problem area for unmarried couples. Why? Because insurance companies have a rule that, in order to purchase life insurance, the beneficiary of the policy (the person who gets the money if you die) must have an "insurable interest". Boiled down, this means nothing more than that the beneficiary must have a relationship to the insured that makes it unlikely that the beneficiary will treat the insured to an early trip to the happy hunting ground in order to collect on the policy. To take an extreme example, no insurance company would be enthusiastic about Joe Gunslinger taking out a policy on the life of Harry Sheriff with himself as beneficiary. Children, spouses, parents and other relatives have long been held to have an "insurable interest" in one another, but traditionally insurance companies have refused to write policies for unmarried couples because they felt that there was no "insurable interest". Apparently they believed that people living together were more likely to slip a little arsenic into the rice pudding than were the married. The result of this rule was that many unmarried couples lied — pretended they were married — in order to get insurance that they couldn't get otherwise. This, of course, played right into the insurance companies' sweaty palms. When one member of the couple died, they often refused to pay on the grounds that there had been a serious misstatement of fact on the insurance application. In many instances courts ruled that they could do this.

Enough history. Where are we now? Many insurance companies now rule that people living together do have an "insurable interest" in one another and will write policies for unmarried couples. Some companies still balk, however, and knowledgeable brokers and agents have a few sleight of hand techniques to get policies accepted. One is to write the policy with another relative as the beneficiary, substituting in the member of the unmarried couple later. This is legal as you have a right to change your beneficiary. Another common device is to list your friend as a fiance. This works as the insurance companies never seem to be interested in the length of your engagement. But insurance companies are still sticklers for truth on applications, so don't represent yourself as married it you aren't. If you already have a policy in which you have wrongly claimed to be married, change it.

**WARNING!** Some companies do try to charge higher rates to unmarried couples. Call a number of companies and compare rates before you buy.

### 2. Insurance on Your Home

Homeowners insurance for unmarried couples used to be difficult to buy, but this is changing rapidly. Traditionally, some companies would write fire insurance for an unmarried couple who were jointly buying a house, but would not write a joint

homeowners policy containing all of the other provisions discussed below. If the unmarried couple wanted full homeowners coverage, they were each asked to buy separate policies. Of course, this cost considerably more and amounted to a form of discrimination against unmarried couples. But you needn't put up with this sort of nonsense; there are now companies that will write homeowners policies for unmarried couples at the same rates married couples get. To find them, call a younger broker in a part of town where a lot of unmarried couples live. He or she should know which companies to approach.

### 3. Renters' Insurance

This is still an area of considerable discrimination in rates. While unmarried renters can each get insurance to cover their personal property easily enough, traditionally there has been difficulty getting one policy to cover both people so as to qualify for lower rates. Happily, several brokers tell us this is changing and it is now possible for unmarried couples to get a joint policy. Shop around.

### 4. Automobile Insurance

We won't give you a complete review of the ins and outs of automobile insurance because state laws vary a great deal. Many states have adopted some form of no-fault insurance, while others have not. Legislation is pending in Congress to impose federal no-fault standards. When the dust clears and some sort of uniformity occurs, we will include comprehensive information here.

Purchasing automobile insurance can be a problem for unmarried couples, but again not to the extent that it was a few years ago. Before issuing a policy, many companies want a complete list of the people who live in the house with the insured. Do they have cars of their own? What are the license numbers, etc? The insurance company wants to run their own check with the Department of Motor Vehicles to be sure that people with bad driving records are not likely to be driving your car. The more your living situation seems to the company to be communal with a lot of people coming and going, the less likely they are to write insurance.

Unmarried couples who each own their own car should have no trouble getting separate insurance. However, if they own one or more cars jointly, there can be problems. Many companies will not insure both people and cars jointly in the same manner as if they were married, but instead will try to write two separate insurance policies listing each person as the primary driver of one of the cars with the other listed as a secondary driver. This approach sounds OK but it isn't. Why? Because a married couple owning two cars would qualify for a second car discount, but an unmarried couple each listing a car in one name with the other person as a secondary driver would not. One way to get around this is to list both cars in one person's name with the other listed as a secondary driver on both. But again, your best bet is to find a sympathetic insurance salesperson, explore all the the angles and then compare prices. Some companies will give unmarried couples the same privileges and rates as if they were married.

## M. SERIOUS ILLNESS

We are often asked what happens if one member of an unmarried couple becomes seriously ill or is involved in an accident and medical authorities need someone to O.K. a treatment decision. Probably this problem is more imagined than real, as doctors will just go ahead and do what they think is best in a genuine emergency, but it is annoying that spouses are routinely consulted, but living together partners are not. Here is a form that may be of some use, both for treatment emergencies and for hospital visitation privileges. We don't guarantee that this sort of authorization will be accepted everywhere, but it is a lot better than nothing. It would also be a good idea to carry a card in your wallet listing the person you live with as your closest friend and asking that they be notified in case of an emergency.

---

### MEDICAL EMERGENCY AND VISITATION AUTHORIZATION

In the event that I am ill, injured or otherwise incapacitated, I hereby authorize _____
(name)
to make all decisions relating to my medical treatment. This includes any necessary x-ray, examination, anesthetic, medical, surgical, or other procedure carried out under the supervision and upon the advice of a physician or surgeon licensed to practice medicine.

Further, I hereby authorize _____
(name)
to visit me at any time in any hospital, convalescent home, or other facility where I may be undergoing treatment.

This authorization is good from _____, 19____
to _____, 19____.

_____          _____
DATE                                             SIGNATURE

(Notarization is optional, but advisable)

---

### 1. Power of Attorney

It is also possible to prepare a formal power of attorney. A power of attorney will be effective only in those states which do not cancel all powers of attorney when a person becomes unconscious or so ill they can't make decisions. About half the states now recognize "durable powers of attorney" which are valid even though the person signing it is temporarily incompetent. Here we only supply a power of attorney form having to do with the event of an illness. In many states, a power of attorney can also be used to give the living together partner power to arrange business affairs of the other. Because this sort of situation can be so variable and state laws vary, we feel you should see a lawyer to prepare this document. In some areas a power of attorney may not work at all and conservatorship or guardship will be necessary. See Appendix for tear-out power of attorney concerning illness and death, or use the one below.

## Power of Attorney and Temporary Guardianship

I, _____, do hereby give _____ Power of Attorney and appoint _____ as Temporary Guardian for the following purposes.

    1. To authorize any and all diagnosis, medical treatment or hospital care which physician or dentist may deem advisable be rendered me.

    2. To advise a treating physician, dentist, or medical personnel as to any diagnosis, treatment, medical procedure or care that might be under consideration for me.

    3. To have first priority to visit me in any facility in the event of injury, illness, incapacity or incarceration.

    4. To receive into his or her possession any and all items of personal property and effects which may be recovered from or about my person by any hospital, police agency, or any other person at the time of my illness or disability.

    This power of attorney and temporary guardianship shall not be affected by subsequent disability or incapacity.

    This appointment shall remain in effect until revoked in writing.


Signed: _____

Dated: _____


## Acknowledgement

State of _____
County of _____
    On _____, 19____ before me, a Notary Public for the State of _____, personally appeared _____, known
_____

(Notarization is optional but advisable)

## N. MISCELLANEOUS RIGHTS AND RESPONSIBILITIES

Increasingly in the last several years, unmarried couples have sought rights and privileges traditionally associated with marital status. Thus unmarrieds have tried to establish that they are "dependents" to qualify for health insurance through their friend's job and have brought unlawful death actions (claiming loss of consortium) when their partner has been killed.* They have also tried to get unemployment benefits when they have had to leave a job and move to be with their living together partner and travel benefits provided spouses through employment, etc. Most of these efforts have not been successful as, generally speaking, courts have allowed business and governmental agencies to treat married and unmarried couples differently. There is little indication this trend will change soon.

---

* At least one California court has granted damages for loss of consortium, *Butcher vs. Superior Court of Orange Co.* 188 Cal. Rptr. 503 (1983). This case is being appealed to the Calif. Supreme Court.

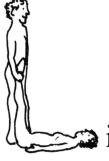 iving Together Contracts and The Law

## A. A LITTLE HISTORY

In the old days, couples who lived together existed pretty much in a legal vacuum as to their legal rights *vis a vis* each other. What little law there was, established that money and property belonged to the one who earned it or originally possessed it or held title to it. Agreements between unmarried people usually were not enforced by the courts, because the courts said that their agreements were based on something called "meretricious consideration." Consideration means the price paid in a contract, meritricious means "resembling a prostitute."

What the old courts were actually saying is that living together contracts were prostitution agreements, and illegal. If one partner agreed to support the other for life in exchange for the other's promise to be housekeeper and companion, many old courts would not enforce this bargain. They would say the contract was really for illicit sex, and illegal contracts can't be enforced. In most states, this left unmarried couples with no way to enforce their agreements.

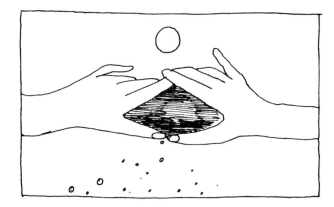

## B. THE MARVIN CASE AND OTHERS: CHANGES IN THE LAW

In 1976, the California Supreme Court decided a case which, partly because of the fame of the litigants, and partly because of the sweeping nature of the court's decision, put living together contracts in the public eye. The *Marvin* case involved actor Lee Marvin, and Michelle Triola Marvin, the woman who lived with him. After they broke up, he supported her for a while, then stopped. She sued him, claiming that in exchange for giving up her career to be a full time homemaker and companion, he had promised he would support her for the rest of her life. The trial court said living together couples couldn't contract with each other. She appealed to the California Supreme Court and they handed down the well-known "Marvin decision."\* The Marvin decision made three significant legal points. It is important to realize that this California decision only establishes the law in that state. However, because some of the legal points in the Marvin case have gained general acceptance beyond California, it is often cited as legal authority throughout the country. To do this is simply not correct, as several of the important elements of the Marvin case have been rejected in many other states.

Let's start by looking at what Marvin decided:

**1. Unmarried couples are not covered by rules that affect the married.** (Or, you're either married or you're not.)

This means only that the California laws on alimony and division of property or divorce do not affect unmarried couples. It doesn't mean that there can't be a court ordered division of property when unmarried couples split up, but only that the specific rules set up by the Family Law Act do not apply. This rule has been widely accepted by other states.

**2. Unmarried Couples May Contract**

The second part of the decision states simply that unmarried couples may make "express" contracts between themselves concerning their property. An express contract is any contract made in words, whether oral or written. The fact that two people live together in a sexual relationship does not make them incompetent to contract with each other regarding earnings and property rights, said the court. However, if the contract is **explicitly** based on the performance of sexual services by one partner, the contract is invalid to that extent. We have never seen this sort of contract, and we doubt the court has either, but it obviously imagines they exist.

---

\* *Marvin v. Marvin,* 557 P.2d 106 (1976)

Almost all states will now recognize **written** contracts between unmarried couples. The major exception is Georgia, where the courts decided that the "immoral" nature of a living together relationship prevented the participants from forming a contract.*

Most states will also recognize **express** oral contracts between living together couples if they can be proved. Proving them, by the way, can be difficult. However, a few states, such as Illinois** and Maryland demand living together contracts be writ-

---

* *Rehak v. Mathis* (1977) 238 S.E. 2d 81. Apparently the courts in this state still will not recognize any contract between unmarried couples.
** *Hewitt v. Hewitt* (1979) 394 N.C. 2d 1204.

ten. This means, practically, that if you are already in a situation where you had an oral contract, and the partnership is over or disintegrated to the extent that you can't get it into writing, you have legal recourse in most states. But again, even where oral contracts are recognized in theory, usually your only proof is your word against your former friend's. The moral: If you and your partner want to be sure to have enforceable legal rights and responsibilities regarding your income or property, the solution is: get it in writing!

### 3. A Court May Imply a Contract From the Circumstances

The really groundbreaking aspect of the Marvin decision was the application to unmarried couples of "implied contract" and "unjust enrichment" theories of law. Implied contract means just what it says; a contract implied from the circumstances surrounding peoples' actions rather than spoken in words. "Unjust enrichment" or "restitutionary" theories of law often apply when one person has contributed something (usually labor) to a venture or project of the other, with the expectation of some benefit in return.

This sort of "equitable" theory was upheld in the State of Washington before the Marvin decision established it as law in California.* However, most courts will NOT recognize implied contracts between unmarried couples,** and even where they will, the problem of proof can be insurmountable, as with oral contracts. If you feel that you contributed economically to your partnership, and should have been compensated, and it is too late to get a written contract, see a lawyer. Otherwise, avoid the whole complicated question by writing down your understanding while you still can.

### C. CONCLUSION: WRITE IT DOWN!

By now, it probably sounds as though we are harping on one theme; reduce your living together agreements to writing. That's exactly our intention. A written contract is the only way to protect both of your rights. AND writing your contract need not be as dreary as you think. (It's certainly better than having courts write one for you), if you approach the task *not* to establish proof for a lawsuit, but to preserve the shared memory of two fair minded people.

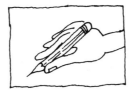

---

* *Estate of Thornton* (1974) 449 P.2d 865. There is also a Connecticutt decision recognizing implied contracts, *Dosek v. Dosek*, 18 CL.J. No. 26.
** Among these is New York, *Morone v. Morone*, 50 N.Y. 2d 481 (1980).

# CHAPTER FIVE

# Contracts

The wonderful thing about contracts is that they can mean as much, or as little, as you want them to. They can cover things as small as a teapot, or as large as a lifestyle. Unlike a legislative act that applies to everyone but fits no one perfectly, contracts belong to you and you may construct them to fit your needs. Legally a contract is no more than a promise (or promises) to do something in exchange for someone else's promise (or promises) to do something in return. Pretty simple. And there is no need to become intimidated by visions of fine print clauses and incomprehensible jargon. These have to do with lawyers and their love for mumbo jumbo and obfuscation, not with contracts themselves.

One reason for a lot of people's general apprehension when it comes to contracts results from the fact that their prior experiences have occurred in situations where they are powerless — insurance contracts, bank loans, major installment purchases, leases, etc. You want or need what the seller is offering and have to accept the one-sided contract that goes with it. Who ever heard of anyone calling up Henry Ford and getting him to add a few months to the warranty? Fortunately, living together contracts need not be written like these standard form monsters. You are free to design the contract to say exactly what you want in words that you can understand. With a little care and attention you should be able to design it to fit like a glove, not a handcuff.

Lawyers notwithstanding, there is nothing illegal about writing a contract in simple English. The simpler it is, the easier it is to understand. For example, you know your friend's name so why not use it instead of calling him the "party of the second part"? When your contract is done, you want to be able to understand it — not have the meaning escape somewhere between the second "wherefore" and the third "pursuant".

## STEP 1 — MAKE YOUR AGREEMENT

Writing your understanding down is basic, but there is something that is even more basic — arriving at a good personal understanding as to what you want to do. When people get married, they automatically receive a contract as to their property — rules and regulations set down by state legislatures and courts in legal codebooks and judicial decisions. People who live together are provided with no prepared-in-advance understanding. They are free to create their own rules and regulations by contract. With the *Marvin* decision and the increasing readiness of courts in every part of the nation to recognize the property rights and obligations of unmarried couples, it is almost essential that people living together have a written understanding of their economic relationship with one another.

We have no magic advice about how to reach an understanding. This is up to you. As two people who live and work together, we arrive at ours more from the flow of what's happening than from a structured business meeting or encounter group approach. But we don't set ourselves up as models for anything. We are as capable of arriving at misunderstandings as the next person. We do suggest, however, that before you try to tie all the details of your agreement down on paper that you carefully read the rest of this book to make sure you understand the basic rules. Oh, and one more thing — don't put off making your contract until you have a fight — the best time to agree is when you are feeling so relaxed with each other that no agreement seems necessary.

## STEP 2 — PUT IT IN WRITING

This is the most important part of this book. If you write your understandings down, all of the complicated remedies described in the discussion of the *Marvin* case in Chapter 3 can be avoided.* If you have a written understanding you are extremely unlikely to ever end up fighting in a courtroom. And if you do, the judge will be interested only in interpreting your written agreement. A court won't normally start inferring and presuming unless you have no written agreement.

From a down to earth, practical perspective, almost nothing gets resolved in court. Those of you who have been through a divorce already know this — those of you who haven't are lucky. Any money or property that exists at the start of a court dispute almost always gets consumed by the lawyers. And then there is the time, emotional pain and bitterness that are so much a part of our adversary domestic relations court process. Have we convinced you? Do you have your pen and paper out? With a written agreement as to who owns what and how property is to be divided if you separate, all of this can be avoided.

---

* No one has put it better than the French legal scholar Beaumanoir in his *Coutumes de Beauvaisis*, written in the year 1283. "For the memory of men slips and flows away, and the life of man is short, and that which is not written is soon forgotten."

## STEP 3 — DESIGN YOUR CONTRACT

There is a wide variety of economic arrangements that can be made by people living together. This freedom and flexibility to order your life in the way you want, free from the traditional institutional rules of marriage, is one of the reasons why living together has become so popular. You can create your agreements to reflect this freedom by carefully designing them to meet your circumstances. Property agreements can be simple or complex, two sentences or twenty pages. Many people live together precisely because they don't want to share their property, while others operate on the assumption that what belongs to one belongs to both. A couple may agree to keep their earnings separate, but compensate one person for services of benefit to the other. They may choose to pool a part, but not all, of their earnings, or form a partnership, or hold property as "joint tenants", or agree to any one of countless other plans. Living together contracts can also include everything that is relevant to the living together arrangement including division of housework, whether or not to have children, the name to be used, property division at separation, and even who takes the dog out for its nightly stroll. However, contracts are normally only enforceable in a legal sense to the extent that they refer to personal property and real property. Provisions relating to children will only be enforced by a court if the court, in its independent judgment, believes that the contract terms are in the best interests of the children (see Chapters 8 and 9). Contract provisions having to do with the personal conduct of the couple are not enforced in practice. Courts will simply not tell you or your friend to put the cap back on the toothpaste or not to piss on the toilet seat.

**REAL PROPERTY NOTE:** We discuss buying houses and other real property in Chapter 7. Real property has its own specialized rules and is usually, but not always handled in a separate agreement. Several sample agreements are set out in Chapter 7.

**MARRIED PERSONS NOTE:** We have gotten many inquiries from people who are living together at the same time one of them is still married to someone else. They want to know if they can legally create a living together contract. In most states there exists a legal provision whereby the property accumulated after a married couple **separates** (a divorce decree is commonly not the crucial point) becomes the separate property of the spouse that acquires it. Therefore, a living together contract would be perfectly valid as to any property accumulated with a living together partner even though one or both partners are still married to someone else. This is almost sure to be true in the states which have made all conduct of consenting adults legal (see Chapter 2).

Valid living together contracts remain valid if the couple later marries at least as to the property acquired prior to marriage while they were living together. However, it is possible that there could still be some problem in states that still outlaw adultery. If significant amounts of property are involved, do some legal research or see a lawyer.

## A. FILL-IN LIVING TOGETHER CONTRACTS

In the Appendix at the back of this book we have included two fill-in, tear-out contracts. One is designed to keep property separate, the other to pool and share it. Read these carefully but don't make any choices until you have read the other alternative contracts in this chaper and the rest of the book with special emphasis on Chapters 3 and 7. The two contracts in the Appendix are fairly thorough and cover most areas of concern to the average unmarried couple. Assuming that one of these reflects many of your concerns, choose it as your basic draft. You are likely to find that you will want to make some additions or deletions based on your circumstances. Fine — here is how to do it.

### ◗ Deletions

Deletions can be handled by simply crossing out and initialing the offending provisions. If you make a number of changes it will be neater to re-type the whole contract. Simply use regular 8 1/2" x 11" typing paper.

### ◗ Additions

Additions are a bit more complicated — you have to write or type out the new provision and add it to the contract. We have left a space before the signatures for you to do this. If you decide not to use this space, it would be wise to cross it out with a large X. When you read through the other examples of living together contracts in this chapter you may find provisions that you would like to add to the basic contract, or perhaps substitute for an existing provision. Go right ahead. Remember, your goal is to create a contract that feels comfortable and right to you.

If your substitutions, deletions and additions begin to eat up the original, you may want to have your finished product checked by an attorney. This is a particularly good idea if you have a lot of money or property. But be careful when dealing with attorneys — many charge outrageous prices and have little experience with the problems encountered by unmarried couples. Do some investigating before you make an appointment and be sure to get the fee set in advance. Remember, you have already done most of the work and you are only asking a lawyer to check it. A fee of $100 should be adequate for this service (see Chapter 12).

### ◗ Signing The Contract

In the Appendix we have provided one copy of each contract. When you have decided which one you are going to use, or have designed your own, xerox your final draft. Both of you should then sign and date both copies of the contract. Notarization is optional unless your contract involves real property and you need to have it recorded at the County Recorder's office. Failure to notarize doesn't make your contract any less legal, but notarization does serve to prove that your signatures are legitimate and not forged in the unlikely event that anyone might question their validity.

### ◗ Relax

One last word. Many people find that filling out or creating a contract like this forces them to deal with the very guts ot their relationship. This is surely a healthy thing to do, but it can also at times be trying. Take your time and don't expect to do the whole job in an evening. Remember too that a good contract normally involves a spirit of compromise and accomodation. If you both feel that you have given up a little more than you received you are probably on the right track. Preparing your contract should be an affirmative act, but it's up to you to make it so. If you get too bogged down in trading this for that and start wondering why you are dealing with all of this legal bullshit, try writing each other a poem.

## B. SHORTFORM PROPERTY CONTRACTS

For those of you who do not feel the need to be as thorough as the agreements in the Appendix contemplate, we have designed simple, one-page statements to the same effect. The rest of this chapter contains contracts designed to fit a variety of lifestyles and circumstances. Read them carefully. You may find something that will work for you.* Let's start with a shortform agreement designed to keep all property separate followed by one which puts it all together.

---

### SAMPLE AGREEMENT (SEPARATE)

Keija Adams and Felix Finnegan agree as follows:

1) That they have been living together and plan to do so indefinitely;

2) That all property whether real or personal owned by either Keija or Felix as of the date of this agreement shall remain the separate property of its owner (if there are a number of valuable items you will want to include an itemization);

3) That Keija and Felix will share their love and good energy, but they agree that the income of each, and any accumulations of property traceable to that income, belong absolutely to the person who earns the money. Any joint purchases shall be made under the terms of paragraph 7 below;

4) That in the event of separation neither Felix nor Keija has a claim upon the other for any money or property for any reason unless there is a subsequent written agreement to the contrary under paragraph 7;

5) That Felix and Keija shall each use his/her own name and will maintain his/her own bank accounts, credit accounts, etc.;

6) That the monthly expenses for rent, food, household utilities and upkeep and joint recreation shall be shared equally;

7) That if, in the future, any joint purchases are made (such as a house, car, boat, etc.) the joint ownership of each specific item will be reflected on the title slip to the property, or by use of a separate written agreement which shall be signed and dated. Joint agreements to purchase or own property shall only cover the property specifically set out in the agreement and shall in no way create an implication that other property is jointly owned.

8) That property owned now, or acquired in the future, as the separate property of either Felix or Keija, can only become the separate property of the other, or Felix and Keija's joint property under the terms of a written agreement signed by the person whose property is to be re-classified.

9) That this agreement replaces any and all prior agreements whether written or oral and can only be added to or changed by a subsequent written agreement.

| | |
|---|---|
| _____ | _____ |
| Date | Keija Adams |
| _____ | _____ |
| Date | Felix Finnegan |

## SAMPLE AGREEMENT (TOGETHER)

Phillip Mendocino and Ruth Alameda agree as follows:

1) That they plan to live together commencing March 1, 19    and to continue to live together indefinitely;

2) That all real and personal property earned or accumulated by either Phillip or Ruth prior to their getting together belongs absolutely to the person earning or accumulating it (it would be wise to include an itemization);

3) That while they are living together all income earned by either Phillip or Ruth and all property accumulated with the earnings of either person whether real or personal, belong in equal shares to both and that should they separate, all accumulated property shall be divided equally;

4) Should either Phillip or Ruth inherit or be given property, it belongs absolutely to the person receiving the inheritance or gift;

5) That the separate property of either Phillip or Ruth covered in paragraphs 2 and 4 of this agreement can become the separate property of the other, or the joint property of both, only under the terms of a written agreement;

6) That should Ruth and Phillip separate, neither has any claim for money or property except as set out in paragraph 3.

_____     _____
Date                                Phillip Mendocino

_____     _____
Date                                Ruth Alameda

## C. AGREEMENTS COVERING JOINTLY ACQUIRED ITEMS

Most people who have consulted us or who have attended our lectures or workshops want to adopt a basic keeping-things-separate approach. Often, however, there will be a major item, or several major items, that they want to own together. As you will see from reading either the contract in the Appendix or the short form contract, we have provided a structure for you to do this. Here is a sample agreement covering a specitic item that you can modify to fit your needs.

---

### AGREEMENT COVERING A JOINT PURCHASE

Cerena Takahashi and Sam Armistead agree as follows:

1) That they will jointly acquire and own a stereo system valued at $900;

2) That should they separate and both want the stereo, they will agree on a fair price and then flip a coin, with the winner keeping the stereo after paying the loser the agreed-upon price;

3) If on separation neither person wants the stereo or if they can't agree on a fair price, it shall be sold to the highest bidder and the money equally divided.

| Date | Cerena Takahashi |
|------|------------------|
| Date | Sam Armistead |

---

Sometimes only one of you will legally make a joint purchase. This can occur because only one of you has good credit or for some other reason. Even though only one name is on the contract with the seller, you may wish to own the property together. Here is a sample agreement to accomplish this:

---

## AGREEMENT

Joseph Benner and Josephine Clark hereby agree that:

1) Joseph has entered into an agreement with Sears, Roebuck and Company to purchase a bedroom set consisting of one king-size bed, one double dresser, two nightstands, and two lamps at a total cost of $900, and

2) Joseph has agreed to pay to Sears said sum in monthly installments of $90 for ten months, due on the first of every month beginning January 1, 19    , and

3) It is the intention of Joseph and Josephine that this bedroom furniture shall be owned equally by both and that both shall pay one-half the cost, and

4) Each shall make one-half the payments on the furniture. Each payment shall be made directly to Sears, on or before the date the payment is due, and

5) Should one person fail to make his or her payment, the other shall have the right to make the payment and the amount of the payment shall be added to the share in the furniture of the person who makes it, and

6) Each shall keep a record of all payments made. All payments shall be made by check or money order, and

7) Upon the death of either, the interest of the deceased in the furniture shall immediately belong to the person surviving. That person shall pay all monies, if any, due and owing on the furniture. If either Joseph or Josephine should make a will, this provision will be incorporated in said will, and

8) If Joseph and Josephine should stop living together, either person may buy the interest of the other in the furniture at a sum agreed upon, taking into consideration the money, if any, still owing on the furniture, and

9) If Joseph or Josephine cannot agree as provided in paragraph 8, the furniture shall be sold. Upon the sale each shall be entitled to one-half the net proceeds realized from the sale unless payments have been made under paragraph 2 of this agreement, in which case each shall be entitled to that percentage of the net proceeds which corresponds to the percentage of the payments he or she has made of the total payments.

_____     _____
Date                                Joseph Benner

_____     _____
Date                                Josephine Clark

---

**NOTE:** If one of you signs a credit agreement to purchase an item, only that person is legally obligated to pay the creditor. This is true even if you and your friend sign an agreement among yourselves to share ownership and payments. Of course, the creditor will take the payments from anyone and properly credit your account, but if a payment is not made, he will go after the person (or persons) whose name is on the account (see Chapter 2).

## D. AGREEMENTS COVERING JOINT PROJECTS

John and Marsha live together. They have no property to speak of, but they have a dream. They want to build their own boat and sail around the world. They foresee that it will take a lot of time, energy and cooperation and they want to protect their vision should any of life's disappointments affect their relationship.

### AGREEMENT

John and Marsha agree as follows:

1) That both desire to construct a 30-foot sailboat to be jointly owned upon completion.

2) That each will contribute $5,000 for the purchase of necessary supplies.

3) That each person will work diligently on the boat (this means at least 20 hours per month).

4) Should they separate, Marsha shall have the opportunity to buy out John's share for an amount of money equal to John's actual cash investment plus $7 per hour for each hour he has worked on the boat.*

---

* There are, of course, other ways to provide for what happens if one person wants out of a deal. The unfinished boat could be sold to the highest bidder and the proceeds divided, a coin could be flipped to decide who gets first right to buy it, etc.

5) At separation, should Marsha decide not to buy John's share under the terms of the previous paragraph, John shall have the opportunity to buy her share on the same terms.

6) Should neither John nor Marsha elect to purchase the other's share of the boat at separation, the boat shall be sold and the proceeds divided equally between the two parties.

7) If either fails to put in 20 hours of work per month for three consecutive months on the boat, the other may buy out his (her) share under the terms set down in paragraph 4.

8) Should either John or Marsha die, the other becomes sole owner of the boat. If either John or Marsha makes a will, this provision will be incorporated in said will.

_____          _____
Date                                  John Mason

_____          _____
Date                                  Marsha Deere

## E. AGREEMENTS COVERING HOMEMAKER SERVICES

Ted is 45 and divorced with custody of his two children. He is a doctor with an annual income in excess of $65,000. Joanne is 38 and also divorced with custody of her child. Her ex-husband consistently refuses to meet his support obligations. Ted and Joanne decide to live together and agree that Ted will earn the money and that Joanne will take care of the three children and of the household on a full-time basis. They are interested in a contract that will protect both of them, providing Joanne with fair compensation for her housework and childcare, but not giving her any rights to Ted's property should they separate.

## AGREEMENT

Ted Corbett and Joanne Lewis agree that:

1) Ted shall continue to work as a doctor with the expectation that he will work a 40-50 hour week and shall have little time or energy to devote to taking care of the home;

2) Joanne will work in the home supervising the children and taking care of all domestic chores including cleaning, laundry, cooking and gardening. Ted will pay Joanne $250 a week for her services over and above the costs of running the home which are set out in paragraph 7.* These payments shall be adjusted from time to time to reflect changes in the cost of living;

3) Ted will make Social Security payments for Joanne as his employee and will pay for complete medical coverage for her and her son, Tim;

4) All real and personal property owned by either Ted or Joanne prior to the date of this agreement shall remain the separate property of its owner (it would be wise to include an itemized list);

5) After the date of this agreement all property owned, earned or accumulated by Ted or Joanne shall belong absolutely to that person earning or accumulating it. The house and its furnishings will be provided by Ted and will be owned solely by him. All property purchased by Joanne with her earnings belongs to her;

6) That property owned now, or acquired in the future by either Ted or Joanne can only become the separate property of the other, or Ted and Joanne's joint property under the terms of a written agreement signed by the person whose separate property is to be reclassified;

7) Ted will provide reasonable amounts of money each month to provide food, clothing, shelter and recreation for the entire family as long as they live together. By doing this Ted assumes absolutely no obligation to support Joanne or her child upon termination of this agreement (see paragraph 9);

(OPTIONAL CLAUSES see Chapter 10 for more information
on separation agreements)

8) Ted and Joanne each agree to assume full responsibility for the other's children in the event the other dies during the time this agreement is in effect. Ted agrees to make provisions for Joanne and the children in his will;**

9) Either Ted or Joanne can end this agreement by giving the other two months' written notice. Joanne will be entitled to severance pay at her current weekly rate of pay for two months for every year the agreement has been in effect. This money shall

---

* These payments may be deducted from Ted's taxes as they are legitimate business expenses. Joanne will have to include them as part of her taxable income, but as she probably has little or no other income, her tax liability, if any, will be small.
** If you wish to include this sort of provision it will be wise to check your contract and your will or other estate planning devices with a lawyer. See Chapter 12.

be paid in a lump sum at the time of separation. Neither Ted nor Joanne shall have any other financial obligation to the other upon separation. (If clause 9 is included, clause 7 will have to be modified.)

| | |
|---|---|
| Date | Ted Corbett |
| Date | Joanne Lewis |

## F. AGREEMENTS COVERING HOUSEHOLD EXPENSES AND PERSONAL IDIOSYNCRASIES

Annie and Clem have been seeing each other for over two years before they decide to live together. Annie is a fashion model and Clem is a private detective. They both have adequate incomes and decide to keep their earnings and property separate.

### AGREEMENT

Annie Auburn and Clem Black agree as follows:

1) That they plan to live together for the indefinite future;

2) Each will use his or her own name;

3) Neither will use the credit of the other and both will maintain separate bank and credit accounts;

4) The earnings and other assets of each shall be kept separate and each shall keep absolute ownership of his or her real and personal property whether accumulated before or after the date of this agreement and shall be responsible for his or her own personal expenses including clothing, medical and dental bills, long-distance telephone calls, entertainment, car, cleaning, laundry, etc., unless otherwise agreed to in writing. If Clem and Annie acquire any property jointly, they shall make a separate written agreement to cover this property and what happens to it if they separate. However, the financial obligations relating to the management of the joint household, which include rent, utilities, food and cleaning supplies, shall be payable using a "joint funds" system which shall work as follows:

Each year on January 1, Clem and Annie will tell one another the amount of their current annual income after taxes (minus any alimoney or child support paid for prior family obligations). The two income figures shall then be added together and a ratio arrived at by dividing the total into Annie's net income and then dividing the total into Clem's net income. Household expenses shall be paid according to this ratio. (For example, if Annie clears $25,000 and Clem $15,000 — they would add these figures together and get $40,000. Then they would divide $40,000 into $25,000 and $15,000 respectively. The result of these equations is that Annie earned close to 60% of the total combined income and Clem close to 40% and the household expenses would be divided accordingly);

5) The separate property of Annie and Clem whether owned now or acquired in the future can only become the separate property of the other, or Clem and Annie's joint property under the terms of a written agreement signed by the person whose property is to be re-classified;

6) Each shall be responsible for domestic tasks.* However, certain daily tasks will be assigned based on the following realities: Annie has no sense for food and cooking while Clem is not too neat and does not require as high a standard of order and cleanliness as does Annie;

    a) Clem will do food shopping and cooking and will take care of all the plants;

    b) Annie will wash dishes and do the cleaning including general straightening, sweeping, dusting and keeping the bathroom in order;

7) Neither Clem nor Annie wants children at this point in their lives. Since the most effective mutually acceptable birth control methods on the market today are female contraceptives, Annie will take responsibility for birth control. However, if in the future a safe and effective oral male contraceptive becomes available, Clem agrees to use it;**

8) In the event that Annie gets pregnant, she will get an abortion which will be paid for jointly;**

9) Clem and Annie agree that each shall make a valid will, revocable upon the ending of this agreement, providing that all of their property will pass to the other in the event of death (see Chapter 11);

10) Either Clem or Annie can terminate this agreement by giving the other a 30-day written notice. Upon separation, each shall take his or her separate property and any jointly held property will be divided according to the separate written joint ownership agreements;

11) Neither Clem nor Annie will have any financial responsibility to support the other after separation.

| Date | Annie Auburn |
|------|--------------|

| Date | Clem Black |
|------|------------|

---

* Agreements to perform domestic tasks are expressions of intention, not contracts enforceable in court.
** Agreements to have or not to have children are only expressions of intention and are not legally enforceable. See Chapter 9.

## G. AGREEMENT DESIGNED FOR STRUGGLING ARTISTS

Terri and Chris have lived together on and off for three years. They decide to enter into a living together agreement which would give each time to pursue her own interests. Terri is a potter and Chris is a musician, but both have had to take ordinary part-time jobs in order to make ends meet. Now they wish to·take turns supporting each other, so that the person being supported can do his or her thing full-time.

---

### AGREEMENT

Terri McGraw and Chris Macklin agree as follows:

1) Each of us will keep whatever property and income from that property we presently hold as of the date of this agreement as our separate property. But any property or income from this property, including salaries or financial returns from artistic pursuits, which either of us acquires from the date of this agreement forward as long as we live together will belong equally to both of us and will be jointly shared. All joint funds will be kept in joint savings and checking accounts;

2) We both agree to take turns working at regular full-time jobs in order to earn enough money for both of us to live on. Terri will work for the first six months of this agreement, and Chris the next six months and so on for alternating six-month periods for the duration of this agreement;

3) All household expenses and personal and medical expenses of both of us will be assumed by the one who is employed at the time the expense is incurred;

4) If one of us wishes to end the living arrangement and the other does not, prior to the dissolution of this agreement, both of us agree to participate in conciliation sessions with a mutually acceptable third party. If, after a minimum of three sessions, one of us still desires to end the agreement, then it will be so terminated. Upon separation, each of us will take our separate property (property we owned prior to living together) and all joint property (property acquired while we lived together) will be evenly divided. No financial or other responsibilities will continue between us after separation.

5) The separate property of either of us (property one of us owned before signing this agreement, or income from that property) cannot become the separate property of the other or the joint property of both without a written agreement signed by the person whose separate property is to be re-classified.


_____          _____
Date                             Terri McGraw

_____          _____
Date                             Chris Macklin

---

63

## H. AGREEMENT FOR PEOPLE IN SCHOOL

Carol plans to be a veterinarian and Bill is an aspiring dentist. To maximize both career opportunities and their personal relationship they decide on a contract with the following provisions:

---

### AGREEMENT

Carol Thayer and Bill Fugimoto agree as follows:

1) That they are living together and plan to continue to do so indefinitely.

2) That all property accumulated by either prior to the date of this agreement (including all income earned by this property in the future) shall be the separate property of its owner.

3) That they will take turns going to school so that the person not going to school can support the other until he/she gets a degree. To decide who will go to school first a coin will be flipped. The loser will be solely responsible for the winner's educational expenses and support for the next four years. When this period is up, the person who goes to school first assumes these same responsibilities for the following four years for the other person. If their living together relationship should dissolve at any time during these first eight years, they stipulate that the financial obligations shall not be affected. This means that if dissolution occurs during the first four years (and Bill has won the coin flip), Carol will continue to pay Bill's tuition and pay him an additional $4,000 per year for living expenses. At the end of the first four years, Bill shall then pay for Carol's tuition for four years and her living expenses at $4,500 per year. If they separate after Carol starts her schooling, Bill will pay Carol's remaining tuition (up to four full years in a school of veterinary medicine) and pay her $4,500 per year in living expenses. All living expenses are to be paid in 12 equal monthly payments.

4) During the first eight years that Carol and Bill live together all of the income and property of either person, excluding gifts and inheritances, will be considered jointly owned by both. The income-producing person will have management and control over the funds. After the first eight years an inventory will be taken of all the accumulated property and it shall be equally divided. Thereafter, each person's earnings shall be his or her separate property and neither will have any rights to any interest in the present or future property of the other. Should Carol and Bill separate before the end of eight years, all accumulated property shall be equally divided according to the fraction of time each has provided the support (if Carol supports four years and Bill two years, Carol is entitled to two-thirds of the property). If a separation occurs, neither person shall have any continuing financial obligations to the other except as set out in paragraph 3 above.

5) Both Carol and Bill will retain their own surnames.

6) If there are children, both Carol and Bill agree to submit to at least three conciliation sessions before ceasing to live together. If a decision to dissolve the relationship is made, both Carol and Bill agree to submit to binding arbitration if they are

unable to reach a mutual decision regarding the issues of child custody, child support and property division. It is the strong conviction of both Carol and Bill that they wish to avoid any battles over custody and support and want to stay away from courts and lawyers if possible.

7) Any change in the ownership status of any property (*i.e.*, from separate to joint or from the separate property of one person to the separate property of the other) shall be done in writing signed by the person making the transfer.

_____     _____
Date                                          Bill Fugimoto

_____     _____
Date                                          Carol Thayer

## I. ENFORCEABILITY OF CONTRACTS

As we have previously stated, agreements between unmarried couples are generally enforceable in a court of law to the extent that they apply to real property, personal property (money, insurance policies, stocks, etc., as well as stereos, cars, ice boxes, etc.) and payment for services. They are generally not enforceable when they involve conduct that normally has little or no monetary value. Thus, if you contract to pay your friend $500 per month for two years in exchange for putting you through school, your agreement will be recognized by a court, but if you contract to feed Nectarine, the pet turtle, every afternoon if your friend gets up early to make the coffee, a judge isn't likely to be very interested if you file a lawsuit saying that your friend overslept.

**WARNING:** No contract will be enforced by a court when one person has taken advantage of (cheated) the other. In living together contracts, courts are particularly strict. Thus, if a rich C.P.A. makes a one-sided contract with a nineteen-year-old who has just moved to this country and has no ability to speak the language or understand business, a court may refuse to enforce it. So if one of you is manifestly more sophisticated than the other, and a considerable amount of property or income is involved, having the less business-wise person see a lawyer for a short consultation before signing would make sense.

**NOTE:** In Georgia there is some doubt that any contract entered into by members of an unmarried couple is enforceable. Why? Because the courts in that state still think it's sinful for people to live together and that allowing unmarried adults to contract about living together somehow encourages the "nasty practice." It is possible that a few tradition-minded judges in conservative areas of the country could follow the lead of Georgia, but the trend is strongly the other way. If you are worried about the state of the law in your area, see a lawyer before signing on the dotted line.

## J. MEDIATION AND ARBITRATION OF DISPUTES

By adding a mediation-arbitration clause to any contract, you free yourself of the need to go to court if a dispute arises. You solve your dispute by following the arbitration procedure that you have set out in your contract. The essential bankruptcy of our overpriced, overcomplicated and time-wasting court system is leading more and more people to prefer this approach which is normally faster, cheaper and less hostile when compared to court. Business has used arbitration to settle disputes for years at least in part as a result of the realization that getting a dispute settled quickly can be as important as who wins and who loses.

Here is a sample mediation-arbitration clause which can be added to any of the written agreements in this book, including the ones in the Appendix. There are many other mediation-arbitration alternatives which you may want to check out yourself at a law library.*

Any dispute arising out of this suit shall be mediated by a third person mutually acceptable to both of us. The mediator's role shall be to help us arrive at our solution, not to impose one on us. If, however, we both agree a mediation approach will not resolve our dispute after we have engaged in three unsuccessful mediation sessions, either or both of us may make a written request to the other that our dispute be arbitrated. The arbitration shall be carried out by three arbitrators, with each of us

---

* See Elias, Legal Research: How to Find and Understand the Law, Nolo Press.

designating one arbitrator and the two designees naming a third. The technical details of the arbitration shall be carried out as follows:

a) The initiating person shall inform the other of the nature of the dispute in writing at the same time that he or she names one arbitrator;

b) Within five days from receipt of this notice, the other person shall reply in writing naming the second arbitrator;

c) The two arbitrator designess shall name a third arbitrator within ten days from the date that the second arbitrator is named;

d) An arbitration meeting shall be held within two days after the third arbitrator is named. Each person shall be entitled to present whatever oral or written agreements he or she wishes and may present witnesses. Neither person may be represented by a lawyer or any third party;

e) The arbitrators shall make their decision in writing within five days after the arbitration hearing. The decision of a majority is controlling;

f) If the person to whom the demand for arbitration is directed fails to respond within the proper time limit by naming an arbitrator, the person initiating the arbitration must give the other an additional five days written notice of "intention to proceed to arbitration." If there is still no response, the person initiating the arbitration may proceed with the arbitration before the arbitrator he or she designated and his or her award shall have the same force as if it had been settled on by the full board of three arbitrators;

g) If the arbitrators designated by the two parties can't agree on a third arbitrator within ten days, arbitration shall be held before three arbitrators appointed by the American Arbitration Association and following their rules;

h) The arbitrators shall be entitled to charge at a rate of $30 per hour (you can change this up or down) for their time in addition to any necessary expenses involved in the arbitration itself. This cost shall be borne by the parties as the arbitrators shall direct as part of their award;

i) The arbitration award shall be conclusive on the parties, and shall be set out in such a way that a formal judgment can be entered thereon in the court having jurisdiction over the dispute if either party so desires.

| _____ | _____ |
| DATE | SIGNATURE |

| _____ | _____ |
| DATE | SIGNATURE |

## K. A LIVING TOGETHER CERTIFICATE

When you go to the marriage license clerk and fill out all of the papers necessary to get married, you are in reality paying the government a tax for permission to live together. There is nothing wrong with this. However, you should be aware that if you ever want to get another permission slip to end the marriage, the fees will be vastly higher.

When it comes to living with your lover, you need no permission slip and you pay no tax. However, there is something in a lot of us that loves certificates. We filled one out and hung it over the stove — half as a joke and half to remind ourselves that we are serious about our relationship. You don't have to get married to get some official-looking papers or certificates — you can make your own. Why not? Papers and ink are cheap and your local printer can doubtless help you make up a wonderfully official-looking (or kooky) certificate for less money than the county clerk will charge. And isn't being independent and creative what living together is all about? We include, at the back of the Appendix, a living together certificate designed by Toni and illustrated by Linda Allison.

# CHAPTER SIX

# Renting and Sharing a Home

## GOBBLEDY-GOOK DEFINED:

EVICT—to legally force someone to move out of an apartment, house, etc. This is accomplished by the landlord suing the tenant and obtaining a court order that the tenant remove himself (or herself) from the premises.

LANDLORD (MALE), LANDLADY (FEMALE), LANDPERSON (NON SEXIST)—the person who owns property which is rented to a tenant.

LEASE (as a noun)—a written agreement by which the landlord agrees to rent certain property for a specified period of time (commonly one year) in exchange for a certain amount of money; the lease may contain many other agreements and restrictions for each party; (as a verb)—to enter into such an agreement. (See Section I, below.)

LEASE

LESSOR—the person who leases the property to the tenant.

LESSEE—a person who has the right to possession of property under a lease.

LIABLE—legally obligated; if a person is "liable," a court can make an order as regards the obligation; for example, liable for the payment of the rent or liable to pay for all damage caused by any person on the premises.

**RENTAL AGREEMENT**

RENTAL AGREEMENT—If you don't have a lease and pay rent, you probably have a rental agreement. This is a contract between a landlord and a tenant whereby the tenant agrees to make periodic payments (usually monthly) of rent in exchange for the right to have possession of certain property. Typically, a rental agreement will contain many other agreements and restrictions for both parties. A rental agreement may be either written or oral (see Section B, below).

SUBLESSEE—a person who leases from a lessee (tenant) rather than from the original landlord. Most leases require getting the permission of the original landlord.

TENANT—a person who rents property.

## A. RENTING A HOME

This is the nitty gritty, isn't it? If you are going to live with someone, you have to go through the mechanics of getting a place. We can't do much to help you find a beautiful, cheap flat right across from a rose garden, but we can give you some hints about the legal implications of dealing with the landlord and each other if you do find it. This chapter is primarily about the special legal problems encountered by people renting together and does not discuss all aspects of landlord-tenant law. The best available general information in this area is found in the *California Tenants' Handbook* (see coupon at back of this book).*

There are all sorts of landlords. Little old men who raise African violets and don't add so well may have rental property right next to that of a large real estate corporation. Obviously, their attitudes toward life (that includes you) will be vastly different. We can, and do, give you a lot of information about your legal rights, but you will have to do the more important job of arriving at a good human understanding of the person with whom you are dealing.

Most landlords are more interested in your money than your morals. As long as you pay rent on time, keep the apartment clean and don't fight with the neighbors, they don't care which beds you sleep in. There are, of course, exceptions — property owners who still refuse to rent to unmarried couples. Some (despite the divorce statistics) base their refusal on the belief that unmarried couples are inherently less stable than married ones. Others don't even try to be logical — they simply will not rent to unmarried couples because they don't like them.

What are your legal rights to rent a place if you are discriminated against? Are unmarried couples given any sort of protection? Since there is no federal law barring discrimination against unmarried couples, it depends on the state, city or county in which you live. Most have no laws barring this sort of discrimination — a landlord can legally refuse to rent to you because you can't produce a marriage license. In the few

---

* This book is also published in a Texas edition, *The Texas Tenants' Handbook*, Nolo Press.

backward states that still make it a crime to live together (cohabitation) this sort of refusal will obviously stand up (see Chapter 2). However, as Victorian attitudes toward living together begin to change, some states such as Wisconsin and California, and a number of cities including New York, Washington, D.C., Seattle, Minneapolis, Philadelphia as well as a number of smaller university cities have banned discrimination based on sexual orientation. However, laws prohibiting discrimination on the basis of sexual orientation are usually, but not always, interpreted by judges as protecting living together couples.* Anti-discrimination laws are pending in many other areas as we go to press. To get up-to-date information for your area, call your local District Attorney's office, or go to the library and get a copy of both state laws and your county and city ordinances. Check the index under "Housing Discrimination."

If you live in an area where there is no anti-discrimination law to protect you, you will have to decide whether you want to confront the landlord with your lifestyle and make an issue of it, or whether you want to try to slide by. Here are some suggestions that others have found helpful:

Do not flaunt the fact that you are not married. Many landlords will not care. Many will assume you are and not ask.   Depending upon your own personality and how conservative an area you are in, you may want to do the old wedding ring routine. It is not illegal to wear a ring that looks like a wedding ring.

In every city and most large towns there are geographic areas where lots of people aren't married. Often this is particularly true near universities. Ask around and go with the flow if possible.

Assume an air of responsibility and respectability (financial and personal references help). This can relax later.

Do not rent from a landlord who obviously disapproves of you or who is likely to disapprove of you when he or she finds out more about your lifestyle. This is especially important if he or she lives nearby. Life is too short for all the hassles you are inviting. Keep looking until you find a landlord whose head is in the twentieth century. It's worth it in the long run.

But what if the landlord asks if you are married? If you say no, you may lose the apartment. If you say yes, what are the consequences? Practically, probably none — if you are otherwise good tenants, the landlord will be unlikely to hassle you. Legally, if the landlord discovers later that you were not married, he or she might have sufficient cause to evict you in some states. There is no chance that a criminal prosecution would result.

How does a woman sign the lease or rental agreement in a situation where you would just as soon have the landlord believe you are married? If both of you are using the same last name, no problem. If you have different names, there are legal implica-

---

* The federal government bans discrimination on the basis of marital status in public housing by regulation of the Department of Housing and Urban Development (Standards for Establishment and Administration of Admission and Occupancy Regulations).

tions. In California, New York and in almost all other states, a person can legally use any name he or she wants, as long as the name is not used for the purpose of fraud and the new name is used consistently. But if Clem Lawrence and Julie Renoir sign a lease or rental agreement as Clem Lawrence and Julie Lawrence and if Julie does not commonly use the name Lawrence, is Julie getting herself into a legal mess? There is almost no legal authority on this point, but our educated guess is there should be no practical problem. If Lawrence and Renoir regularly pay their rent, the landlord has suffered no financial loss.

Worrying about how to sign your name is pretty dismal, isn't it? However, as society becomes more tolerant of varying lifestyles, the problem should become less frequent. In the end, "good business" will probably win over "good morals" and landlords will resign themselves to renting to those who can pay at the first of each month without regard to their participation, or non-participation, in civil ceremonies. Hopefully, that day is almost here.

## B. LEASES AND RENTAL AGREEMENTS

There are three common methods of renting property:

❷ The Lease — a written lease normally provides for a payment of a specific rent for a specific period of time (typically one year). Most leases also contain a long list of rules and regulations governing occupancy.

❷ The Written Rental Agreement — a written agreement which provides that rent be paid periodically (usually once a month) in exchange for the right to live on the property for the same period. A rental agreement differs from a lease in that the agreement may be ended by either party or the rent raised on very short written notice (usually 30 days). As with a lease, there are normally written rules and regulations which are part of the agreement.

❷ Oral Rental Agreement — the same as a written rental agreement, but nothing is written down. Even with an oral agreement you need a **written** notice (normally 30 days) to terminate the tenancy in California, New York and most other states.

Before signing anything, carefully examine the fine print rules and regulations (covenants) section of your lease or written rental agreement. Many of these rules are extremely restrictive and many are downright illegal. This is because many of the lease forms are out-of-date and still contain provisions that have been outlawed. For example, many lease forms purport to give the landlord the right to evict you immediately without getting a court order should you fail to pay rent on time. This is illegal — only a judge has the legal authority to order that you be moved out. We don't have the space here to list all illegal lease provisions, but if you see something that rubs you the wrong way, check it out; unmarried couples will particularly wish to check for a clause prohibiting "immoral behavior". In states where living together is legal this sort of clause is now meaningless, but in states that still outlaw cohabitation it could cause a problem if the landlord tries to use it to evict you. It would be a good idea to ask the landlord to cross out any "immoral behavior" language. If he or she refuses, it is probably a good indication that you would be happier renting elsewhere.

**IMPORTANT:** Keep copies of all leases, rental agreements and communications with your landlord in a safe place just in case a misunderstanding does develop. In dealing with landlords it is wise to act in a friendly, courteous manner and hope for the same treatment in return; at the same time you should be prepared for the worst, if it happens. As in dealing with people generally, you can normally catch more flies with honey than by hitting them over the head with a mallet.

## C. MOVING IN TOGETHER

### 1. Legal Obligations Of The Tenants To The Landlord

If both Julie and Clem enter into a lease or rental agreement (written or oral), they are each on the hook to the landlord for **all** rent and **all** damage to the apartment. It makes no difference that Julie used Clem's last name when she signed the lease, she is still personally liable to the landlord for **all** rent and damages.

**EXAMPLE 1:** Clem and Julie rent a place using the names Clem and Julie Lawrence and both sign a rental agreement providing for a $500 total monthly rent. They agree between themselves to each pay one-half. After three months Clem refuses to pay his half of the rent (or moves out with no notice to Julie and the landlord). In either situation Julie is legally obligated to pay all the rent as far as the landlord is concerned. Clem, of course, is equally liable, but if he is unreachable or out of work, the landlord will almost surely come after Julie for the whole amount. Since Clem and Julie have rented under a month-to-month written rental agreement, Julie can cut her losses by giving the landlord a written notice (30 days in most states) of intention to move. She can do this even if Clem is lying about the place, refusing to pay or get out.

**IMPORTANT:** If either Clem or Julie ends up paying the landlord more than his or her fair share of the rent, the person who paid too much has a right to recover from the other. If payment is not made voluntarily, this can best be done in Small Claims Court.*

**EXAMPLE 2:** The same fact situation as Example 1, except that this time there is a lease for one year. Again, both partners are independently liable for the whole rent. If one refuses to pay, the other is still liable unless a third person can be found to take over the lease, in which case both partners are off the hook from the day that a new tenant takes over. Because of the housing shortages in most parts of the country, it is reasonably easy to get out of a lease at little or no cost, by simply finding an acceptable new tenant and steering him or her to the landlord. A newspaper ad will usually do it. The landlord has an obligation to limit his or her damages (called "mitigation of damages" in legal slang) by renting to a suitable new tenant as soon as possible. Should the landlord fail to do this, he/she loses the legal right to collect damages from the original tenants.

### 2. Legal Obligations Of The Tenants To Each Other

People living together usually have certain expectations of each other. Sometimes it helps to write these down. After all, you expect to write things down with the landlord almost as a matter of course, so why not do the same with each other? Nothing that Clem and Julie agree to among themselves has any effect as far as the landlord is concerned, but it still may be helpful to have something to refresh their own memories, especially if the relationship gets a little rocky. Here we give you a

---

* See *Everybody's Guide To Small Claims Court*, Warner, Nolo Press.

sample agreement which only covers a rented living space. Many unmarried couples will prefer to incorporate this type of provision in a more comprehensive living together contract such as those discussed in Chapter 5.

---

## AGREEMENT

Julie Renoir and Clem Lawrence, upon renting an apartment at 1500 Peanut Street, Falfurrias, Texas, agree as follows:

1. Julie and Clem are each obligated to pay one-half of the rent and one-half of the utilities, including the basic monthly telephone charge. Each person will keep track of and pay for his or her long distance calls. Rent shall be paid on the first of each month, utilities within ten days of the day the bill is received.

2. If either Julie or Clem wants to move out, the one moving will give the other person and the landlord 30 days' written notice and will pay his/her share of the rent for the entire 30 day period even if he/she moves out sooner.

3. No third persons will be invited to stay in the apartment without the mutual agreement of both Julie and Clem.

4. If both Julie and Clem want to keep the apartment but one or the other or both no longer wishes to live together, they will have a third party flip a coin to see who gets to stay. The loser will move out within 30 days and will pay all of his or her obligations for rent, utilities and for any damage to the apartment.

Here is an alternative for Number 4

4. If both Julie and Clem want to keep the apartment but no longer wish to live together, the apartment shall be retained by the person who needs it most. Need shall be determined by taking into consideration the relative financial condition of each party, proximity to work, the needs of minor children, if any, and (list any other factors important to you). The determination shall be made by a third party who both Julie and Clem agree (in writing) is objective. The determination shall be made within two weeks after either party informs the other that he or she wishes to separate. After the determination is made, the person who is to leave shall have two additional weeks to do so. The person who leaves is obligated for all rent, utilities and any damage costs for 30 days from the day that the original determination to separate is made.

_____     _____
Date                                   Julie Renoir

_____     _____
Date                                   Clem Lawrence

---

## D. MOVING INTO A FRIEND'S HOME

Perhaps just as common as two people looking for their home together is for one person to move in with the other. This can be simple and smooth where the landlord is relaxed and sensible, but can raise some tricky problems and is not recommended where the landlord is a neanderthal idiot who despises unmarried couples. The best advice we can give you when it comes to getting into arguments with idiots is, don't. It makes far more sense to use the same time and energy looking for a place to live where the landlord is pleasant.

In some situations where the landlord is not in the area or is not likely to make waves, it may be sensible simply to have the second person move in and worry about the consequences later. But is this legal? Is a tenant required to tell his landlord when a second person moves in? It depends on the lease or rental agreement. Read the agreement carefully. If no mention is made as to the number of persons allowed in the apartment, use your own discretion and knowledge of your landlord. Some don't care or (like parents) would prefer not to know.

Although moving in with no notice to the landlord is often the easiest thing to do, we suspect that it is commonly not the most sensible. The landlord will probably figure out what is going on before long and may resent your sneakiness more than he or she resents your living with someone. We advise you to:

❷ Read the lease or rental agreement to see how many people are allowed to live on the premises and if there are any restrictions. Sometimes additional people will be allowed for a slight increase in rent. Many landlords who do have their heads in the twentieth century will not care whether you are married, living together or joined by the toes with rubber bands, but will expect to collect more money if more people live in their rental unit.

❷ Contact the landlord to explain what is happening. If you can't do this in person, you might send a letter such as this:

```
                                        1500 Peanut Street, #4
                                        Falfurrias, Texas

                                        June 27, 19___


Smith Realty
10 Jones Street
Falfurrias, Texas

Dear Sirs:

    I live at the above address and regularly pay rent to your office.  As
of July 1, 19___, there will be a second person living in my apartment.
As set forth in my lease I enclose the increased rent due which now comes
to a total of $500.  I will continue to make payments in this amount as
long as two people occupy the apartment.

    Should you wish to sign a new lease to specifically cover two people,
please let me know.  My friend, Julie Renoir, is regularly employed and
has an excellent credit rating.


                                        Very truly yours,



                                        Clem Lawrence
```

**REMEMBER:** A written rental agreement can be terminated on short notice (30 days in most states) without any reason being given. Thus, a landlord who wants to get rid of you can do so easily unless you have a lease or live in a city which has a rent control law requiring "just cause for eviction." However, in our experience, if you have a good payment record and are cooperative, it is not likely that the landlord will bother putting you out even if he/she prefers people who have mumbled "until death do us part." If you live in one of the areas where discrimination on the basis of marital status is illegal (see Section A above), the landlord can't legally put you out because you are living together. If he/she tries to do so, you should file a complaint with the local or state agency charged with enforcement of the anti-discrimination law. Of course, the landlord may make up some phony reason to get rid of you to disguise his or her real reason. If you suspect this, file your complaint and let the landlord try to explain why he/she found you to be an adequate tenant while you were living alone and wants to evict you only after you began living with someone. If the landlord files an eviction action in court you will have to make your case to the judge.

If you have a lease, you are probably in a little better position to bargain with the landlord if a friend moves in. This is because, to get you out before the lease expires, he/she would have to establish that you have violated one or more lease terms.  If your lease has a provision allowing occupancy by only one person, your landlord probably has the right to terminate your tenancy if a second person moves in without his or her permission. However, if he or she accepts rent with the knowledge that you are living with someone, many courts would hold that he/she can no longer enforce that right. If the lease simply says that the premises shall not be used for "immoral or illegal purposes", it is highly questionable whether the landlord can terminate the lease simply because you are living with someone, unless you are in a state which still makes cohabitation illegal. If the matter were pursued as far as a court eviction in such a state (which is unlikely), the answer would probably depend on the biases and prejudices of the judge. In any case, the landlord could not be sure of winning and would probably hesitate to go through the time and expense of an eviction action if you continued to pay your rent and otherwise were a cooperative tenant. Of course, the landlord can wait until your lease runs out and simply refuse to renew it. His/her refusal would be legal unless you were living in an area that prohibits discrimination on the basis of marital status and you could show that his or her reason for refusing to renew the lease was because you were not married.

### 1. What Is The Legal Relationship Between Person Moving In And Landlord?

If Julie moves into Clem's apartment, what is the relationship between Julie and Clem's landlord? Is Julie obligated to pay rent if Clem fails to pay? What if Clem moves out, but Julie wants to remain? If Clem ruins the paint or breaks the furniture, does Julie have any obligation to pay for the damage?

The answer to these questions is that Julie starts with no legal rights or obligations regarding the rent, or the right to live in the apartment. She has entered into no contract with the landlord.* Clem is completely liable for the rent and also for damage to the premises whether caused by Julie or himself, because he has entered into a contract which may be in the form of a lease, written rental agreement or oral rental agreement. If Clem leaves, Julie has no right to take over his lease without the landlord's consent.

Julie can, of course, enter into a lease or rental agreement contract with the landlord which would give her the rights and responsibilities of a tenant. This can be done by:

❷ Signing a new lease or rental agreement which specifically includes both Clem and Julie as tenants.

❷ Making an oral rental agreement with the landlord. Be careful of this one as an oral agreement can consist of no more than a conversation between Julie and the landlord in which she says she will pay the rent and keep the place clean and he says OK. There may be some legal question as to whether an oral agreement between Julie and the landlord is enforceable if there is still a written lease or rental agreement between the landlord and Clem which doesn't include Julie, but it is our belief that most judges would bend over backwards to give Julie the rights and responsibilities of a tenant if she seemed to be exercising them.

---

* Of course, if she damages the property, she is liable just as a visitor, a trespasser, or a thief who caused damage would be liable.

❶ The actual payment of rent by Julie and its acceptance by the landlord especially if it is done on a fairly regular basis. As in the preceding paragraph, this would set up a month-to-month tenancy between Julie and the landlord and would mean that either would have to give the other a written notice (30 days in California, New York and most other states) of intention to end the tenancy.

**IMPORTANT:** Rental agreements, leases, evictions, etc. can get fairly complicated and confusing. If you get into a real problem area, see the *California Tenants' Handbook*, which contains much useful information applicable to all states. Also, you a might consider seeing a lawyer for a one-time consultation. This need not be expensive and you can then decide whether you want to pursue the dispute (see Chapter 12).

Should the situation ever arise that Clem wants to move out and Julie remain, it is important that the legal relationships be clarified. Clem should give the landlord written notice of what he intends to do at least 30 days before he leaves. If he does this, he is off the hook completely in a written or oral rental agreement situation. If a lease is involved and Clem is leaving before it runs out, he is still OK because the landlord has a legal duty to take steps to limit his/her loss as much as possible (mitigate damages). This means finding a new tenant to pay the rent. In our example, as long as Julie is a reasonably solvent and non-destructive person, the landlord would suffer no loss by accepting her as a tenant to fill out the rest of Clem's lease. If the landlord refuses Julie without good reason, Clem is still legally off the hook and any loss is legally the landlord's problem, not his.

(For use if you have a rental agreement)

```
                                        1500 Peanut Street, #4
                                        Falfurrias, Texas

                                        June 27, 19___



Smith Realty Company
10 Jones Street
Falfurrias, Texas

Dear Sirs:

    I live at the above address and regularly pay rent to your office.  On
July 31, 19___  I will be moving out.  As you know, my friend, Julie Ren-
oir, also resides here.  She wishes to remain and will continue to pay
rent to your office on the first of each month.

    We will be contacting you soon to arrange for the return of my damage
deposits of $300, at which time Julie will give you a similar deposit.
If you have any questions, or if there is anything we can do to make the
transition easier for you, please let us know.

                                        Very truly yours,


                                        Clem Lawrence
```

```
                                        1500 Peanut Street, #4
                                        Falfurrias, Texas

                                        June 27, 19___


Smith Realty
10 Jones Street
Falfurrias, Texas

Dear Sirs:

     I live at the above address under a lease which expires on October 30,
19___.  A change in my job makes it necessary that I leave the last day
of February.  As you know, for the last six months my friend, Julie Renoir,
has been sharing this apartment.  Julie wishes either to take over my
lease or enter into a new one with you for the remainder of my lease term.
She is employed, has a stable income and will, of course, be a responsible
tenant.

     We will soon be contacting your office to work out the details of the
transfer.  If you have any concerns about this proposal, please give us
a call.



                                        Very truly yours,



                                        Clem Lawrence
```

## 2. What Is The Legal Relationship Between Person Moving In And Person Already There?

Alas, it seems all too common that big-brained monkeys go through violent changes in emotional feelings. A relationship that is all sunshine and roses one minute may be more like a skunk cabbage in a hurricane the next. Sometimes, when feelings change, memories blur as to promises made in happier times and the nicest people become paranoid and nasty. Suddenly, questions such as "whose apartment is this, anyway?" may turn into serious disputes. We suggest that when feelings are relaxed (preferably at the time that the living arrangement is set up), both people make a little note as to their mutual understandings, either as part of a comprehensive living together arrangement or in a separate agreement. If this is done in a spirit of making a writing to aid the all too fallible human memory, it need not be a heavy experience. We include here an example that you might want to change to fit your circumstances.

# AGREEMENT

Julie Renoir and Clem Lawrence make the following agreement:

1. Clem will move into Julie's apartment and will give Julie one-half of the monthly rent ($250) on the first of each month. Julie will continue paying the landlord under her lease and Clem will have no obligation under the lease.

2. Clem will pay one-half of the electric, gas, water, garbage and monthly telephone service charges to Julie on the first of each month. Julie will pay the bills.

3. Should Clem wish to move out, he will give Julie as much written notice as possible and will be liable for one-half of the rent for two weeks from the time he gives Julie written notice. Should Julie wish Clem to move out, she will give him as much written notice as possible, in no case less than two weeks. In any case of serious dispute, it is understood that Julie has first choice to remain in the apartment and Clem must leave on her request.

_____          _____
Date                                     Julie Renoir

_____          _____
Date                                     Clem Lawrence

**IMPORTANT:** If you get into a serious dispute with your friend involving your shared home and have no agreement to fall back on, you will have to do the best you can to muddle through to a fair solution. Here are a few ideas to guide your thinking:

☯ If only one of you has signed the agreement with the landlord and that person pays all the rent, then that person probably has the first claim on the apartment, especially if that person occupied the apartment first. The other should be given a reasonable period of time to find another place, especially if he or she has been contributing to the rent and/or has been living in the home for any considerable period of time.

☯ If you have both signed a lease or rental agreement and/or both regularly pay rent to the landlord, your rights to the apartment are probably legally equal, even if one of you got there first. Try to talk out your situation letting the person who genuinely needs the place the most stay. Some people find it helpful to set up an informal mediation proceeding with a neutral third person who will listen to the facts before making a decision. If you do this, make sure that the mediator is not a close friend as the person who loses is likely to have hard feelings. Lean over backwards to be fair about adjusting money details concerning such things as last month's rent and damage deposits. Allow the person moving out a reasonable period of time to find another place. **We have found that the best compromises are made when both people feel that they have gone more than half way.**

◗ Each person has the right to all his or her personal belongings. This is true even if they are behind in his or her share of the rent. Never lock up the other person's property.

◗ It is a bad idea to deny a person access to his or her home except in the most extreme circumstances. If you are going to lock a person out, you should also be ready to sign a formal police complaint because it may come to that if your former friend tries to get in by using force. In most cases, except where a person has no right to live on the premises (has not paid rent, has not signed a lease, has not been living with you long), locking a person out is not legal and you can be sued for damages.


## E. DEPOSITS

Getting cleaning and security deposits returned can be a problem for all tenants - not just the unmarried. **To avoid deposit trouble and to handle it when unavoidable you must have good documentation.** By this we mean making a written and photo-graphic record of what the place looks like at the time you move in and then again when you move out. Witnesses - people you know who would be willing to examine your place and then speak out if necessary - are also extremely valuable.

Let's assume now that Clem and Julie move into a rented flat and pay $400 ($200 each) for cleaning and security deposits. What should they do to be sure that they will get those deposits back?

**STEP 1:** First, they should document any problems that exist when they move in. Dirty conditions, damaged rugs or appliances, and scratched walls or floors are exam-ples of conditions that should be noted. The best way to do this is to fill out the landlord-tenant checklist which is included at the end of this chapter. If the landlord doesn't wish to do this or drags his or her feet, Julie and Clem should be on notice that self-protection is essential. They should have a friend or better yet, friends, check the place over and take pictures of offending conditions. The person taking the pictures should write his or her name and the date on the back.

**STEP 2:** Before Clem and Julie move out, they should invite the landlord over to discuss any conditions that might lead to misunderstandings about deposit return. Clem and Julie don't have to leave the place exactly as they found it — part of their rent is to cover normal wear and tear. If there is a problem over and above what might be considered normal — say Julie burned a counter top with an iron — Clem and Julie should get all of their deposits back less the cost of replacing the counter top. If the top was already somewhat damaged from other causes, this should be taken into consider-ation. Assuming that Clem, Julie and the landlord do come to an agreement, they should write it down and sign it. This can be done as part of the same landlord-tenant checklist mentioned in Step 1 or in some other form.

Now and then a tenant gets advance warning that a landlord never returns de-posits voluntarily. This could come from a former tenant, or perhaps even directly when the tenant tries to have a reasonable conversation with the landlord. If you are in this situation, you may wish to take affirmative steps to protect yourself. This is particularly true if you plan to move out of town so that suing later in the local Small Claims Court would be difficult or impossible. Perhaps the simplest way to protect yourself is to withhold the payment of the last month's rent, or that portion of the last month's rent which equals the deposits. If you do this, be sure that you notify the landlord in writing of what you are doing and make sure that you do, in fact, have the place clean and undamaged when you leave. Here is a sample letter:

```
                                        1500 Peanut Street, #4
                                        Falfurrias, Texas

                                        June 1, 19___


Smith Realty
10 Jones Street
Falfurrias, Texas

Dear Sirs:

    As you know, we occupy apartment #4 at 1500 Peanut Street, Falfurrias,
Texas and regularly pay rent to your office.  As we notified you previous-
ly, we will be moving out on July 15, 19___.

    In speaking to other tenants in the building, we have learned that
from time to time, the return of cleaning deposits has been the subject
of disputes between your office and departing tenants.  Accordingly,
we have decided on the following course of action.  Instead of sending
you the normal $500 rent check for June rent, we are sending you a check
for $600 to cover rent for both June and July and are requesting that you
apply our cleaning and damage deposit of $400 to cover the rest of the
rent owed for this period.

    We will leave the apartment spotless.  We have no intention of causing
you any loss or other problems.  If you should doubt this, or want to dis-
cuss this matter further, please give us a call so that we can make an
appointment to check the apartment over.  We think you will be satisfied
that we are dealing with you honestly and in good faith and that the apart-
ment, which is clean now, will be spotless when we leave.


                                        Very truly yours,



                                        Julie Renoir
                                        Clem Lawrence
```

**STEP 3:** If Clem and Julie move out and have no understanding with the landlord, they should be very careful to document the condition of the premises. After they clean up, they should again get friends to inspect the place and take pictures. It is also wise to keep copies of receipts for cleaning materials.

Clem and Julie should receive their deposits back within a maximum of two weeks after moving out. If they don't, they should first write a letter and then sue in Small Claims Court. The letter would look like this:

---

800 Walnut St.
Pampa, Texas

August 1, 19___

Smith Realty Co.
10 Jones St.
Falfurrias, Texas

Dear Mr. Anderson:

   On July 15, 19___ we vacated the apartment at 1500 Peanut Street, #4. As of today we have not received our $400 cleaning and security deposits.

   We left our apartment clean and undamaged, paid all of our rent and gave you proper notice of our intention to move. In these circumstances, it is difficult to understand your oversight in not promptly returning our money.

   Perhaps your check is in the mail. If not, please put it there promptly. Should we fail to hear from you in one week, we will take this matter to court.

Very truly yours,


Julie Renoir
Clem Lawrence

---

If this doesn't work, the next step is to go to Small Claims Court. In most states, the amount that can be sued for is at least $1,000 which should take care of most deposit cases. But Clem and Julie shouldn't just assume that they will win automatically. The landlord may show up claiming that they left the place a mess. To counter this they will need their pictures, witnesses and cleaning receipts (see Steps 1-3 above). Julie and Clem might present their case in the court something like this:*

---

* In most states no one occupies the witness box in Small Claims Court. All testimony is given from a table which faces the judge.

JULIE: Good morning, your Honor, my name is Julie Renoir and this is Clem Lawrence. From May 15, 19__ until July 15, 19__, we lived at 1500 Peanut St., #4 here in Falfurrias. When we moved out, the Smith Realty Co. refused to refund our $400 cleaning and security deposits even though we left the place spotless. We carefully cleaned the rugs, washed and waxed the kitchen and bathroom floors, washed the insides of the cupboards and the windows.

CLEM: Your Honor, I can testify that everything Julie said is true. We worked a full day to get that place really clean. I would like to show you some pictures that were taken of the apartment the day we moved out. These were taken by our neighbor, Mrs. Edna Jackson, who is here today and will testify. Also, I would like to show you these receipts for a rented rug shampooer and waxer plus receipts for other cleaning supplies. They total $22.00. I don't have anything else to add except that Mrs. Jackson and Ms. Kimura are here to testify.

After the witnesses are sworn in and give their names and addresses, their testimony should be brief and to the point.

MRS. JACKSON: Julie and Clem asked me to check their place on Peanut St. over on July 15, the day they moved. It was very clean and neat. I took those pictures that you looked at, your Honor — the ones with my name on the back. I would have been delighted to move into a place as clean as that.

MS. KIMURA: Your Honor, I didn't take any pictures, but I did help Clem and Julie clean up and move out and I can say the place was spotless. I know because I did a lot of the work, including helping with the windows, cleaning the bathroom, putting that smelly oven cleaner on, etc.

# CHECKLIST

The following is a summary of the condition of the premises at

_____, California,
on the dates indicated below.

| | CONDITION ON ARRIVAL | CONDITION ON DEPARTURE |
|---|---|---|
| **LIVING ROOM** | | |
| Floors & Floor Covering | | |
| Drapes | | |
| Walls & Ceilings | | |
| Furniture (if any) | | |
| Light Fixtures | | |
| Windows, Screens & Doors | | |
| Anything Else | | |
| | | |
| **KITCHEN** | | |
| Floor Covering | | |
| Stove & Refrigerator | | |
| Windows, Screens & Doors | | |
| Light Fixtures | | |
| Sink & Plumbing | | |
| Cupboards | | |
| | | |
| **DINING ROOM** | | |
| Floor & Floor Covering | | |
| Drapes | | |
| Walls & Ceilings | | |
| Furniture (if any) | | |
| Light Fixtures | | |
| Windows, Screens & Doors | | |
| | | |
| **BATHROOM(S)** | | |
| Toilet(s) | | |
| Sink(s) | | |
| Shower(s) | | |
| Floor, Walls & Ceiling | | |
| Light Fixtures | | |
| Windows, Screens & Doors | | |
| | | |
| **BEDROOMS** | | |
| Floors, Floor Covering | | |
| Walls & Ceiling | | |

| | | |
|---|---|---|
| Furniture (if any) | | |
| Windows, Screens & Doors | | |
| Light Fixtures | | |
| | | |
| **OTHER AREAS** | | |
| Floors & Floor Covering | | |
| Windows, Screens & Doors | | |
| Walls & Ceilings | | |
| Furnace | | |
| Air Conditioning (if any) | | |
| Lawn, Ground Covering | | |
| Patio, Terrace, Deck, etc. | | |
| Other | | |

Checklist filled out on moving in on _____, 19____, and approved by

_____ and _____.
       Landlord                                                              Tenant

Checklist filled out on moving out on _____, 19____, and approved by

_____ and _____.
       Landlord                                                              Tenant

# uying a House

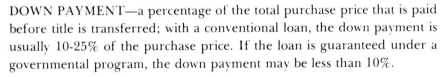

GOBBLEDY-GOOK DEFINED:

>CLOSING COSTS—costs associated with buying a house; these costs include realtor fees, recording fees, notary fees, penalties for paying off a loan early, past due taxes, etc.
>
>CONVENTIONAL LOAN—a loan, normally made by a bank or savings and loan company, that is not guaranteed by FHA, VA, or some other governmental agency.
>
>DEED OF TRUST—a kind of mortgage used in some states
>
>DOWN PAYMENT—a percentage of the total purchase price that is paid before title is transferred; with a conventional loan, the down payment is usually 10-25% of the purchase price. If the loan is guaranteed under a governmental program, the down payment may be less than 10%.

DOWN PAYMENT

>DEED—the legal document by which one person or persons transfer title (recorded ownership) to real property to another person or persons. If the transfer is by a *grant deed,* the person transferring title makes certain guarantees or warranties as regards the title. If the transfer is by *quitclaim deed,* the person transferring does not make any guarantees, but simply transfers to the other person all the interest he has in the real property.
>
>ESCROW—in real estate jargon, the process by which two parties deliver documents or money to a third person (escrow agent) who then completes delivery; for example, the seller will deliver a deed to the third person; the

DEED

buyer or his agents will deliver the money to the same third person. When the third person has received all the money and the deed and other necessary documents, he delivers the deed to the buyer and the money to the seller. CLOSING OF ESCROW refers to the time when all documents and money have been delivered.

ESCROW

FHA—Federal Housing Authority.

INDENTURE—a fancy word for written contract or agreement.

MORTGAGE—Since people rarely have the cash to purchase a home they end up borrowing most of it—this is called taking a mortgage. Technically, it is the security interest that a seller or lender retains in property where recorded ownership (title) has been transferred to a buyer, but the buyer has not paid the whole purchase price. In practice, it is common for a financial institution to pay off the seller immediately and become the mortgage holder; as a verb—to convey or place property under mortgage.

## A. FINDING A HOUSE

There may come a time when you and your friend decide to purchase a house or other real property. For many of us property ownership is symbolic of rootedness, of having a sense of place and belonging. Most societies, including our own, have honored the acquisition of land and the process of building with ceremonies, often spiritual. Even though this planet has been here five and a half billion years, and, measured against such an immensity of time, the concept of owning land is laughable, in our human time frame it can make great sense. Perhaps if we think of ourselves as stewards of our land and living spaces, rather than owners, we can connect both to our need for foundation and place as well as recognizing that, in a larger view, our presence on the land (or in the house) is a momentary one and that we owe something to those who are yet to come as well as to the land itself.

Sadly, as the earth has become more crowded and building supplies scarcer, the availability of decent living spaces has decreased. Even in the past few generations we have seen the death of America's founding dream — each family with a good home on good land and room to grow. Now many of us rent from necessity and many others express their desire to be homeowners with cooperative apartments or condominiums. Still, more than in most parts of the world, the possibility of home ownership exists despite high land, construction, and interest costs and property taxes that are so exorbitant that they might as well be called rent.

Here we will give you both general information about buying a house and specific ideas that unmarried couples will find of value. From time to time we will suggest that legal advice on some detailed point would be helpful. Before seeing a lawyer, however, we suggest you read Chapter 12.

In some states, sales of real property (land and/or buildings) are handled in close consultation with an attorney. In most, a real estate broker handles all of the transactions and attorneys are not normally involved. In all the states, the individual has the right to handle the purchase or sale himself and should certainly make sure he has the best possible deal. There are several paperback books on the market which discuss buying and selling a house without a real estate broker. With a good deal of study, effort, and care, buyer and seller working together doing things themselves can save at least 10% of the sale value of real property. Because the financial community (banks, real estate brokers, title companies, lawyers, etc.) is interrelated, it often happens that one or more of these interest groups will make it difficult for you if you don't patronize all of them. Difficult is not the same as impossible, however, and if you are interested, check with your bookstore or library for helpful materials. You want to look for books that relate to your state particularly, as opposed to those that pretend to be of national scope.

For the unmarried couple, buying a house generally involves four distinct steps:

1. Finding the house.

2. Financing the purchase.

3. Transferring ownership (taking title to the house).

4. Working out a sensible agreement between the buyers.

Finding a house normally involves no special problem for the unmarried couple. The overwhelming majority of sellers will not care about your marital status. If you use a realtor, you are particularly unlikely to have problems as the realtor will not receive his commission unless he sells the house, and is thus generally willing to encourage the owner to sell to anyone. But what happens if, despite good business and common sense, the owner of a house or condominium refuses to sell to you because you are not married? In most states nothing happens because there are no laws stating that it is illegal to discriminate on the basis of marital status in the sale of real property. Such discrimination is illegal in California, Wisconsin, Oregon, Washington, D.C. and a number of smaller cities.* Check the state and municipal codes in your area under "Housing Discrimination" or "Real Estate Practices."

**NOTE:** In Chapter 2 we discuss the fact that cohabitation (living together in a relationship that includes sex) is itself a crime in some states. Does this mean that an unmarried couple will have difficulty buying a house in these states? No. As noted, the anti-cohabitation laws are not enforced and it seems no more difficult for an unmarried couple to buy property in these states than in the others.

You may have read that some local communities have enacted zoning ordinances preventing more than a specified number (usually 2-4) of unrelated persons from living together (excepting household help, of course) in an attempt to eliminate communes from their neighborhoods. While some legal scholars feel that such ordinances discriminate against unmarried persons and are unconstitutional in that they deny equal protection of the laws to such persons, the United States Supreme Court does not agree. In the case of *Village of Belle Terre v. Boraas*, 416 U.S. 1 (1974) the Supreme Court held that anti-group living ordinances are constitutional. This means that they allowed the village of Belle Terre to say that no more than two unrelated people could live in the same house. But what does all of this mean for unmarried couples? Very little — the Supreme Court has approved zoning ordinances that prohibit **more** than

---

* Several other cities and counties have enacted gay rights ordinances which prohibit discrimination in housing on the basis of sexual orientation. The wording of some of these ordinances is broad enough to protect both straight and gay couples. Such ordinances exist in Los Angeles, Philadelphia, Washington, D.C., a few smaller cities and the State of Wisconsin.

two unrelated people from living together: The Court has not said that it is constitutional for a neighborhood or town to ban unmarried couples. Indeed, the language of the *Belle Terre* case seems to indicate that, if faced with such a case, the Court would prohibit a community from discriminating against unmarried couples.

Several state Supreme Courts have interpreted their own constitutions or laws to prohibit local communities from discriminating against groups. The New Jersey Supreme Court declared that a zoning ordinance that prohibited more than **four** unrelated individuals from sharing a housing unit violated the New Jersey Constitution, *State v. Baker*, (1979) 405 A. 2d 368. The California Supreme Court has issued a similar decision.*

## B. FINANCING YOUR HOUSE

Very few people are able to pay cash for a house. Most of us have to borrow money and accept the conditions imposed by the lender. Sometimes the realtor will tell the buyer that he can arrange for the financing of the house. This can be helpful, for the realtor may be able to persuade a bank or other lending agency to loan you money when you would not otherwise be able to obtain a loan. However, realtors often have working relationships (business habits) with certain lending insitutions that can result in your being referred there even though better interest rates are available elsewhere. Often, too, the realtor may simply be lazy and not know the practices of banks other than the ones he usually deals with. So before accepting an offer of help, shop around and compare the interest rates and fees of different lending institutions. Several careful research studies have shown that lending practices, fees**, and interest rates can

* *City of Santa Barbara v. Adamson*, (1980) 164 Cal Rptr. 539.

** Yes, most banks charge you a fee for the privilege of borrowing money from them. This is in addition to the interest you pay for the use of money.

vary considerably even within a small geographical area. For most people a house is the most expensive purchase they will ever make, and the property should not be bought or financed without careful attention to all details (interest rates, repairs, taxes, etc.).

How much can you afford to pay for a house? People who have thought carefully about this generally state that the purchase price should not exceed three times the annual gross income of a family. This is probably a good rule for unmarried couples as well. A larger purchase price may well result in house payments that are unrealistically high. In figuring the purchase cost you must add not only the cost of the house itself, but also the cost of the structural repairs you will be required to make (in some cases the seller makes these repairs and the cost is reflected in the purchase price), the closing costs*, and at least one-half of the redecorating costs you plan to incur in the first year. Some lending institutions may require repairs to be made before the loan will be granted. Financial institutions are also concerned with the portion of net income that it will take to pay mortgage installments and taxes — generally they will not loan unless the monthly total is less than 33% of net monthly income.

## 1. Financing: What's Involved

In most cases you must pay a cash down payment for at least 10-25% of the purchase price and the closing costs. The rest of the money for the purchase of the house will be loaned to you by a bank or other lending institution which will retain the "mortgage" or similar legal interest in the property until you pay the entire purchase price (this may take 25 years or more). When you buy a house, you must be able to afford the monthly payments on the house as well as the initial down payment. The charts below show monthly payments that will have to be made on various mortgage loans at different rates of interest for various lengths of time. These are all fixed rate mortgages. As you can see, a 1% difference in the interest rate can result in a large difference in the total amount of money you end up paying for a house. A $30,000 loan can easily cost you $100,000 in total payments over a 30-year period.

---

In order to pay off a loan of $30,000 in 25 years you will have to make the following monthly payments at the specified interest rate:

| | | | |
|------|----------|-----|----------|
| 10% | $272.70 | 13% | $338.35 |
| 11% | 294.03 | 14% | 361.13 |
| 12% | 315.97 | 15% | 384.25 |

---

* These can easily equal a couple of thousand dollars and the buyer and seller must agree ahead of time as to how they will divide the costs.

In order to pay off a loan of $40,000 in 25 years you will have to make the following monthly payments at the specified interest rate.

| | | | |
|---|---|---|---|
| 10% | $363.50 | 13% | $451.13 |
| 11% | 392.05 | 14% | 481.50 |
| 12% | 421.29 | 15% | 512.33 |

In order to pay off a loan of $50,000 in 25 years you will have to make the following monthly payments at the specified interest rate.

| | | | |
|---|---|---|---|
| 10% | $454.35 | 13% | 563.92 |
| 11% | 490.06 | 14% | 601.88 |
| 12% | 526.61 | 15% | 640.42 |

In order to pay off a loan of $70,000 in 25 years you will have to make the following monthly payments at the specified interest rate:

| | | | |
|---|---|---|---|
| 10% | $636.10 | 13% | 789.49 |
| 11% | 686.08 | 14% | 842.49 |
| 12% | 737.26 | 15% | 896.59 |

You must also take into account the fact that you will be paying taxes and fire insurance as well as monthly loan payments. In some cases these costs will be added to and included in the monthly payments you make, with the lending institution then purchasing the insurance and paying the taxes for you. Often lending institutions don't purchase the most reasonably priced insurance; sometimes they charge a fee for paying the property taxes. Normally, it is cheaper to handle these things yourself. If you are directly responsible for making the payments, the lending institution will surely retain the right to make the payments (and add the cost to the mortgage) if you fail to do so.

**EXAMPLE:** Felix and Keija are an unmarried couple. Felix is a teacher and earns $26,000 yearly before taxes and other deductions are subtracted from his checks. After deductions he brings home $1600 per month. Keija manages a restaurant and earns $21,000 every year before deductions. She brings home $1300 per month. Each of them has a savings account of about $12,000. Each of them intends to continue working and sees a gradual increase in income in the future. Their annual gross income is $47,000. Taking both incomes together, they could afford a house with a cost in the range of $100,000-$130,000 without strain.

Felix and Keija find a house that is advertised for sale for $100,000. They offer $90,000 to the seller and the seller agrees to sell for $95,000. Felix and Keija accept this "counteroffer" and then find a bank that will loan them 80% of the purchase price at the rate of 12% for 25 years. The taxes are $950 per year and the fire insurance will cost $250 per year. The seller will pay for all repair work that must be done on the structure. Felix and Keija will want to repaint the inside of the house and remodel the kitchen. They plan to do the painting themselves; the supplies will cost $800, and they have an estimate from a contractor that remodeling the kitchen will cost $6,000. Their cost of obtaining title to the house (closing costs) is $3,500.

| | |
|---|---:|
| Total cost of house equals: | |
| Purchase price | $95,000 |
| Closing costs | 3,500 |
| Half of redecorating costs | |
| ($3,000 + $400) | 3,400 |
| | $101,900 |

| | |
|---|---:|
| Total monthly payments equal: | |
| Loan payment (25 year loan | 842.58 |
| at 12% interest on 80% of | |
| $80,000, or $64,000) | |
| Monthly taxes ($950 ÷ 12) | 79.17 |
| Monthly fire insurance | 20.83 |
| ($250 ÷ 12) | |
| | $942.58 |

The monthly payments will be $942.58, or slightly over 32% of Felix and Keija's total net monthly income. In addition, Felix and Keija must pay a down payment of 20% of the purchase price. This comes to $19,000 plus closing costs of $3,500, or a total of $21,500. Keeping all these costs in mind, plus the costs of maintenance on the home, they have a big decision to make.

Suppose Felix and Keija decide that they are willing to invest their money in this house. The next problem facing them is how to obtain a loan for the 80% of the purchase price that they can't pay in cash.*

**WARNING:** In shopping around for the money to finance your house, beware of institutions which will loan you money at a fluctuating rate of interest. Some loan agreements are structured so that, while the borrower makes regular payments on the

---

* Sometimes a seller is willing to carry the mortgage himself, but most commonly he/she wants his or her money, or most of it, right away, making it necessary to get outside financing. Sometimes a lending institution will not lend the buyer enough to completely pay off the seller even when the loan is added to the down payment. This means that a second mortgage to make up the difference is necessary. Sometimes a seller will provide the second mortgage directly. If not, it may be necessary to borrow from family or friends.

house, the rate of interest he pays changes according to some criterion outside the loan (such as the prime interest rate or the Consumer Price Index). The idea behind this kind of loan is that the lending institution profits because its money is always loaned out at the optimum rate, and the borrower profits because, if the prevailing rate goes down, he will automatically start paying a lower rate of interest without having to obtain another loan. Of course, the borrowers have had their monthly payments increased drastically and a few where couples have been priced out of their own home. We believe the average borrower is better off with the certainty of a fixed rate even if this means paying a slightly higher rate to start.  However, if you do choose a non-fixed mortgage be sure the amount it can fluctuate has some limit or cap. Never accept a mortgage that can fluctuate without limit.

**In deciding whether or not to loan money on real property, all financial institutions look carefully at two factors: (1) the value of the property itself; and (2) the personal financial circumstances of the borrower.** Some lenders are more concerned with the value of the property on the theory that their investment is well protected, even if the borrower fails to make his payments, as long as the property is worth more than their loan. Other lenders put more emphasis on the financial situation of the borrower, only lending to people in excellent financial shape. Institutions which look more to the credit of the borrower do so because they do not want to be bothered with the legal complications of regaining property and the hassle of collecting overdue payments. They simply want to be sure that the money comes in every month.

Traditionally it has been difficult for unmarried couples to get mortgage loans. Financial institutions have long adopted the attitude that they are unstable. People who work in banks tend to be conservative and to think that everyone who doesn't follow all of society's traditional formalities (like marriage) can't be trusted to pick up candy wrappers, discipline their children, or more important, pay their bills. In practical application this attitude used to mean that banks would not lend jointly to both members of an unmarried couple. They usually insisted that the loan be solely in the name of the person with the highest income, and would only consider that person's income in measuring ability to repay. In effect, the bank was pretending that the unmarried couple didn't exist. More than one couple was told that, if they wanted both incomes considered and wanted both names on the loan and deed, they would have to do one very simple thing — get married.

Fortunately, hostile attitudes toward lending to unmarried couples have been mellowing over the last few years. Much of this change for the better is traceable to the fact that so many more unmarried couples are buying houses, but much is also the result of the Fed.Equal Credit Opportunity Act, which forbids credit discrimination based on sex or marital status. This act means that a woman, whether single or married, is entitled to receive credit on the same basis as a man with a similar credit profile.* Banks now cannot act as if unmarried couples don't exist. In preparing this

---

* Women who believe that they have been discriminated against should contact the nearest regional Federal Reserve Board office (for bank-related problems) or the nearest regional Federal Trade Commission (for non-bank related problems).

book we talked with a number of bankers. Most indicated (at least to us) that they had no negative attitudes toward unmarried couples, but we did find hostility among a few. "We know we have to deal with them, but we don't have to like it," one man told us. There is an old saying: "Don't try to push a river, especially if it's going in the wrong direction." Check with unmarried friends to see who in the banking or real estate business is going your way.

When Felix and Keija get a loan (mortgage) it means two things: the real property itself is liable (can be foreclosed on) to pay off the debt, and Felix and Keija are personally obligated to pay the entire amount. Assuming that the loan is made to Felix and Keija together, **both** are on the hook to pay it all back. Felix can't excuse his failure to pay by claiming that Keija has not made her share of the payments. **Let's say it again, because it is important:** Felix and Keija are each independently liable to repay the whole debt. Indeed they are both required to pay back the loan even if they transfer (sell) the property to a third person who agrees to make the payments **unless** the bank agrees to release them from their obligation and allows the new person to "assume" the mortgage. Even if something happens to the house (fire, flood or other catastrophe), Keija and Felix are still legally on the hook to repay the bank loan. But because banks know that people don't like to pay for things that no longer exist, they will require that Keija and Felix take out insurance that will at least cover the amount of the bank loan.

Now let's look at some other real estate financing possibilities.

With today's high interest rates, it is often essential that you find a seller who will give you a loan to finance a portion of the purchase. (In real estate jargon this is called "carrying paper.") Rather than requiring that you make a down payment and then raise all the rest of the purchase price from a bank or other lender, the seller agrees that you can pay some of the sales price in the form of a promissory note, or by assuming the seller's mortgage payments. Thus the seller receives some of his or her cash over time, rather than all at once.

If the seller needs all of his or her cash at once, he or she won't be willing to carry your paper. But many sellers aren't so pressed for cash and will work out a more flexible payment plan. For instance, if the seller is planning to put the money in a bank, lending it to you instead makes great sense if you offer to pay a higher interest rate. The seller's loan to you is very secure because, like the bank, the seller will get a mortgage on the house in return for the loan and can foreclose if you fall behind in your payments.

Let's presume for a moment that you are infatuated with a home selling for $120,000. What with your savings, borrowing from parents or friends, and getting a loan on your car, you can raise $30,000. You need $90,000 more (plus closing costs). The seller has owned the home for a few years and has a $50,000 mortgage on it at 9 percent interest. Here are several different possible methods of financing your purchase.

*Plan A:*

Offer to purchase the home for $120,000 cash as follows:

$30,000 down payment;

$90,000 at current bank interest rates;

If interest rates are 14%, the payments will cost you $1,066.

*Plan B:*

Pay the sales price of $120,000 as follows:

$30,000 down payment;

$50,000 by assuming the seller's old mortgage at 9%; payments of $402 per month over 25 years.

The seller lends you the $40,000 remaining, taking a note and a second mortgage, and you make monthly payments of $381 including interest at, say, 11%, with a final (balloon) payment for the remaining balance due in seven years. (The monthly interest payment rate and the time of the balloon payment are open to negotiation.) Total monthly payments equal $783.

*Plan C:*

Pay the sales price of $120,000 as follows:

$30,000 cash down;

$15,000 is loaned to you by the seller at 11%, for seven years; monthly payments are $143; the loan is secured by a second mortgage;

$75,000 new bank loan at current bank interest rates. (If interest rates are 12%, the payments will cost you $771 per month.)

Total monthly payment equals $914.

*Plan D:*

To make it more attractive to the seller, you offer $2,000 above the sales price.

Pay the sales price of $122,000 as follows:

$30,000 cash down;

$50,000 by assuming the seller's old mortgage at 9% (over 25 years), with payments of $402 per month.

$42,000 loan from seller, in exchange for a second mortgage and a note; monthly payments are $400 per month, including interest at 11%, with a final (balloon) payment due in seven years.

Total monthly payments equal $802.

To summarize: The sales price is only one consideration in any home purchase deal. Terms, such as the amount of down payment, interest rates, etc., can be at least as important.

## 2. Your Home as Investment and Tax Shelter

Now the good news! There are many financial benefits to owning a home. This is especially true in times of rapid inflation. Not only will homeownership provide you with a place to live but with any luck at all your investment will go up in value while you live there. In addition, Congress has concluded that Americans should be encouraged to own homes and has written the tax laws to create significant tax advantages for homeowners.* These rules state that all interest that you pay on your mortgage, as well as the cost of your property taxes, are deductible from your ordinary income for tax purposes. This means that when you determine the amount of income you must pay taxes on, you can first subtract these costs. By way of comparison, you get no such deduction if you are renting — even if, as is usual, your rent is used to help pay the landlord's taxes and mortgage interest payments.

Another tax advantage granted to real property owners is the special treatment given any profit or gain realied when the property is sold. If you own your home for over a year** and make a profit when you sell, the profit is labeled as "capital gain" rather than as "ordinary gain." This is a big advantage, as "ordinary gain" is combined with your other income and taxed at regular rates, while "capital gains" are taxed at only 40 percent of ordinary rate.

**EXAMPLE:** If you earned $25,000 from your work and won $10,000 at the race track, you would have a taxable income of $35,000. But if you made $10,000 on the sale of your home (or real estate) and this money qualifies as "capital gain," only 40 percent of that profit is counted. Forty percent of $10,000 is $4,000, so your taxable income would only be $29,000. In other words, 60 prcent of the profit on the sale of your real property is ordinarily not taxed.

Homeowners also qualify for another tax advantage. (Now you know why tax accountants often say that people with good incomes can't afford not to own real property.) If you sell your home and buy another within 18 months, and you put your profits from the first home into the second one, you are allowed to postpone paying taxes on the gains until you sell your second home. This means that you can keep trading up to more expensive properties and postpone paying taxes on your accumulated profits while you are doing it. Or to express it in a different way, you can use money that you would otherwise have had to pay taxes on for a larger investment.

Finally, there is a tax rule that helps older folks whose homes have skyrocketed in value. It works like this. Any time after you are 55 years old, you may sell your home and not pay any taxes on the first $100,000 profit. You can do this one time only. Again, as with all the rules we discuss here, be sure to check the current status of all tax rules before acting.

### 3. F.H.A. Financed Housing

The Federal Housing Authority (F.H.A.) guarantees loans on certain types of houses, typically tract or development homes build after World War II. This means that financial institutions will lend to people (often with a low down payment) who might not otherwise qualify for a home loan. The Authority also administers some special programs in which they loan money, sometimes with a subsidy, to low-income persons.

---

* Actually, the tax advantages go to *owners* of real estate generally.
** The time you must hold the property has varied recently, as Congress tinkers with the capital gains law to "better engineer society."

You may have heard that it is difficult for unmarried couples to qualify tor F.H.A. guarantee or loan programs. Until a few years ago, this was true — F.H.A. would lend to unmarried couples, but would only count the income of the male when making a determination as to whether the family met their income requirements. Since people turn to F.H.A. to start with because they can't qualify for conventional financing, this was a little like saying to a starving person, "I will give you a terrific supper, as soon as you fatten up a little."

F.H.A. now assures us that they no longer discriminate and that unmarried couples are judged by the same criteria that their licensed brothers and sisters are judged by. This means that the agency will count the income of both people when determining financial ability whether people are married or not.

## C. TAKING TITLE TO THE HOUSE

When you purchase a house together (or any other property, for that matter), you should both use your correct names. These are the names by which you are generally known and which appear on most of your identification documents, such as your driver's license, passports, credit cards, etc. These need not be the same names that appear on your birth certificates. For example, Keija should take title as Keija Adams if she had adopted Keija as her legal name. This is true even though her birth certificate says Carolyn.

At the time you purchase your home, you will have to decide on how you want to "legally" take title. In most states your choices are in "one person's name", as "joint tenants" or as "tenants in common". Let's pause for a moment to translate these terms into English.

### 1. In One Person's Name Only

You probably will not be interested in this alternative if you are buying a house together, because unless you have executed a separate agreement (see Section D4, this chapter) it means that the person whose name appears on the deed is the sole owner. Sometimes having only one name on the deed seems momentarily desirable for some reason such as preserving welfare or food stamp eligibility. **Beware!** You may sacrifice a large, long-term gain for a small, short-term one. This is because the person whose name is on the deed is "presumed" to be the sole owner. If you later split up, or the person whose name is on the deed dies, the other person may find that he or she has no rights even though he or she has contributed to the house payments. But shouldn't it be possible for the person whose name isn't on the deed to show that he or she is really part owner from the facts of the relationship? Perhaps — some states allow the presumption that the person who has his or her name on the deed is the sole owner to be rebutted if the facts are strong enough. But even if this is possible it involves the expense and time of going to court.*

---

\* Those wanting to do more research in this area will want to look at the case of *Antoine v. Thornton*, **81** Wash. 2d 72, **499** P. 2d 864 (1972).

## 2. Joint Tenancy

Taking title to a piece of real property "as joint tenants" means that legally the joint tenants share in property ownership and each has the right to use the entire property.* If one joint tenant dies, the other(s) automatically takes the deceased person's share without the necessity of any probate proceedings. Indeed, when one joint tenant dies, the property can go only to the surviving joint tenant(s), even if there is a will to the contrary. If one joint tenant sells his or her portion to a third party, this ends the joint tenancy. The third party and the original joint tenant become "tenants in common" (see below). Joint tenancy is not appropriate to a situation where a house is owned in unequal shares, only to those where each joint tenant owns the same individed portion as does the other(s).

## 3. Tenants In Common

Tenants in common are also each entitled to equal use of the property, **but if one party dies the other party does not take his share unless this has been specified in the deceased person's will.** If there is no will, the deceased's share in the property goes to the nearest blood relative under the intestate succession laws of the state where the property is located (see Chapter 11).* If this were Aunt Tillie in Omaha, Nebraska, the surviving member of the unmarried couple and Aunt Tillie would now be tenants in common. Therefore, whether you and your partner buy the house as joint tenants or tenants in common will probably depend on who you want to inherit your share of the

---

*   Sometimes one member of an unmarried couple buys a house and then is tempted to put the house in "joint tenancy" with his or her friend, so that the friend will have it if the purchaser dies. Think before you do this — by putting the house in "joint tenancy", you are probably making a gift of one-half of it to your friend. If you later split up, you will probably be unable to get the half you gave away back. You will probably be better off to keep the house in your name and make a will in favor of your friend. If you wish, the will can always be changed later.

** A surviving tenant in common might argue that he or she get the deceased person's interest in the property because of the existence of an oral or implied contract under the theory of the *Marvin* case (see Chapters 4 & 11). While this sort of argument might work (if the existence of such a contract can be proved, and if you are in a state where such contracts are recognized), where personal property is involved, it seems to us to be even more difficult where real property is concerned. Why? Because a written agreement already exists (the co-tenancy deed), and we believe that courts will be reluctant to change deeds on the basis of oral testimony.

property.* One word of caution: DO NOT take title to the house as "husband and wife", or as "Felix Finnegan and his wife, Keija". This can only lead to legal problems in the future. Tenancy in common can be used where people own a house together, but in different shares (see D below).

## D. CONTRACTS BETWEEN UNMARRIED PEOPLE BUYING HOUSES

It is all very well to list the various common ways of taking title to a house. But how does listing yourself as "tenants in common", or "joint tenants" answer such questions as "who gets to keep the house if we split," or "what do we do if one of us puts in twice as much for the down payment as the other," or "what happens if one of us already owns a house and the other wants to move in and share ownership?" The answer to these questions is that you need to make a written understanding (a contract).

**NOTE FOR PEOPLE WHO HATE CONTRACTS:** Many people will prefer not to make a contract but rather to fly by the seat of their pants, sure that their love and respect for each other will insure a soft landing. As we discussed in Chapters 4 and 5, this can be dangerous. Where valuable pieces of property such as houses are involved, it is particularly necessary to write something down. If you do split up and you **mutually** agree to a solution different than the one in your written contract, fine. You can tear up the old contract and get on with the new. However, if your relationship ends with more of a bump than you guessed, and you find it hard to communicate, you will still have your written understanding to fall back on.

A house contract can be simple. After reading this section, you may conclude that you can prepare it yourself, either as part of a comprehensive living together contract or as a separate agreement. However, houses are major investments and you don't want to make an agreement that either doesn't solve all your problems or makes them worse. So if your agreement is complicated, you will be wise to have it checked by someone who is familiar with the legal problems encountered by unmarried couples. This doesn't mean that you should take a full wallet and a vague basketful of problems to a lawyer. It does mean that you should do as much work as possible yourself and only use the lawyer to help you with particular problem areas (see Chapter 12).

**Unmarried couples who are jointly buying a house will usually find that the things they want to write down as part of a contract fall into the following subject areas** (to make this easier to understand, let's resurrect Felix and Keija):

1. *Who keeps the house if Felix and Keija split up and both want it?*
2. *How do Felix and Keija decide the value of the house if they split up?*
3. *Assuming that Felix and Keija split up and a decision is reached that one of them will keep the house and buy the other out, how is the transfer accomplished?*
4. *If one person invests more money in the house than the other, how can the unequal shares be reflected in a contract?*

---

* There are inheritance tax consequences associated with different kinds of ownership. This book does not deal with these tax problems as they are not of major significance to people of average income. If you are very wealthy or are buying property with a high value, you would be wise to discuss these problems with a tax attorney or an accountant.

*5. If one person moves into a house already owned by the other, what legal steps can be taken to protect both parties?*

We can't give you the answers to every possible variation on all of these subject areas, but we hope at least to give you a structure for thinking about your situation and for dealing with a lawyer if necessary. Before we examine each of these five questions, let's first set out a simple sample contract to give you an idea of what you are aiming at. Under Parts 4 and 5 of this section we will discuss several more complicated agreements.

---

### SAMPLE HOUSE PURCHASE CONTRACT

Keija Adams and Felix Finnegan agree as follows:

1. That they will purchase the house at 1400 Beverly St., San Jose, California for $120,000 and will take a title to the home as tenants in common.

2. That Keija and Felix will each contribute $20,000 to the down payment and will each pay one-half of monthly mortgage and insurance costs.

3. Keija and Felix will each be responsible to pay one-half of all property taxes and one-half of any costs for needed repairs.

4. In the event that Keija and Felix decide to separate and both want to keep the house, a friend shall be asked to flip a coin within 30 days of the decision to separate. The winner gets to purchase the house from the loser provided that he (she) pays the loser the fair market value (see paragraph 5) of his or her share within 90 days. When payment is made, the house shall be deeded to the person retaining it.

5. The fair market value of the house shall be determined at any time by either the written agreement of Keija and Felix, or, if this is impossible, by appraisal. The appraisal shall be carried out as follows: Keija and Felix shall each designate one licensed real estate broker or salesperson who is familiar with the neighborhood where the house is located to make an appraisal. The two appraisers so designated shall jointly agree on a third licensed real estate broker or salesperson to make a third appraisal. The three appraisals shall be averaged to arrive at the fair market value of the house. The fees of the three appraisers shall be paid in equal shares by Keija and Felix.

6. In the event of the death of either Keija or Felix, the survivor shall have the right to purchase the interest of the deceased person by paying the fair market value (see paragraph 5) of that interest within 200 days of the date of death.

7. This contract is binding on our heirs and our estates.

(Notarization is necessary if you wish to record this agreement.)

_____

Now let's look at variations. This material isn't difficult, but you will want to read it through several times to be sure that you understand it completely.

## 1. Who Keeps The House If Felix And Keija Split Up?

Let's assume now that Keija and Felix have been living together for three years prior to the time that they decide to buy their house. In the year prior to the house purchase there has been some tension between them — Keija thinks that Felix should be less promiscuous, and Felix gets furious because Keija never cleans the kitchen and squeezes the toothpaste from the wrong end. Both have agreed to work out these problems and plan to continue living together for the indefinite future, but there are just enough clouds on the horizon for both to realize that staying together "until death do us part" is not inevitable. While they are communicating well, both want to write something down so that if they do break up, there will not be a lot of paranoia about who gets the house.

Here are the most common types of contract clauses that would solve this problem. Keija and Felix will have to decide which best suits their circumstances.

a) "In the event that the couple (or one of them) decide(s) to separate, Felix shall keep the house and pay Keija the fair market value of her share within sixty days of the decision to separate." (Of course, this agreement can be reversed by reversing the names.)

or

b) "In the event that the couple (or one of them) decides to separate, the house shall be listed for sale within thirty days of this decision, and the proceeds of the sale equally divided after all costs of sale and mortgage debts are paid."

or

c) "In the event that the couple (or one of them) decides to separate and both want to keep the house, a friend shall be asked to flip a coin within thirty days of the decision to separate. The winner gets to purchase the house from the loser provided that he (she) pays the loser the fair market value of his or her share within ninety days of moving out."

or

d) "In the event that the couple (or one of them) decides to separate and both want to purchase the share of the other, they shall jointly agree in writing on a third person to act as a mediator-arbitrator to help them decide who shall be entitled to purchase the house from the other. The mediator-arbitrator shall meet with both

*Felix and Keija at least three times in an effort to help them to arrive at their own decision." (Add on arbitration clause - see Chapter 4).*

or

*e) "In the event that Felix and Keija (or one of them) decide(s) to separate at a time when one of them has physical custody of minor children, the person with physical custody of the children shall have the first choice to stay in the house. The person staying in the house shall pay the other the fair market value of his or her share within ninety days of separation.*

## 2. How Do Felix And Keija Decide The Value Of The House If They Split Up?

When people split up, they often believe that legally they must sever all ties between one another. While at times this may be emotionally desirable, it is not legally required. Keija and Felix may legally continue to own their house or other real property together as long as they wish to, even if they split up fifteen minutes after the house is purchased. However, it is common to find that when people separate and a decision is made for one to stay in the house and the other to leave, the person leaving wishes his or her share of the equity in cash. Sometimes it is possible for the person staying in the home to pay immediately, sometimes not. But before you reach this question, you must determine the value of the house. Here is a contract provision that takes care of this simply and fairly:

*a. "If Felix and Keija (or one of them) decide(s) to end the relationship and to divide the equity in the house, the value of the home shall be determined as follows:*

*1) By mutual written agreement at any time;*
*2) Or, if agreement is not possible, by appraisal. The appraisal shall be carried out as follows: Keija and Felix shall each designate one licensed real estate broker or salesperson who is familiar with the neighborhood where the house is located to make an appraisal. The two appraisers shall jointly choose a third licensed real estate broker or salesperson to make a third appraisal. The three appraisals shall be averaged to arrive at the fair market value of the house. The fees of the three appraisers shall be paid in equal shares by Keija and Felix.*

## 3. Assuming That Felix And Keija Split Up And A Decision Is Reached That One Of Them Will Keep The House And Buy The Other Out, How Is The Transfer Accomplished?

Here are some alternatives:

*a) "Within ninety days after Felix and Keija decide to separate, the person staying in the house shall pay to the person leaving his or her share of the net equity at which time the person leaving shall deed his or her share of the house to the person staying."*\*

---

\* Before you know what the equity is you must agree on the fair market value of the home. This is where the appraisal come in. Once you know the fair market value, you subtract the amount of the mortgages (or deeds of trust as well as costs of sale) to arrive at the new equity.

b) *"Within ninety days after Keija and Felix (or one of them) decide(s) to sepa-rate, the person remaining in the house shall pay to the person leaving one-half (one-third or one-fourth or whatever amount works for you) of his or her share of the net equity. The person staying in the house shall also give the person leaving a second mortgage (or deed of trust) for the remainder of his or her share. The mortgage (deed of trust) shall be for a term of five years (three, six or whatever works for you) and shall be payable in equal monthly installments. This mortgage (deed of trust) shall be recorded at the County Recorder's office.*

**NOTE FOR PARENTS:** If the person staying in the house is going to be primarily responsible for the care of the couple's children, it may be particularly difficult for him or her to raise cash to pay the other off for the house. In this situation it may be wise to establish the value of the respective interests in the house at the time of separation, but not require the person staying (the parent with custody) to pay the other until the children reach the age of majority, or the family moves or the house is sold. This can be done by the person leaving deeding the house to the parent with custody in ex-change for a mortgage which doesn't fall due until the appropriate time in the future.

### 4. Owning a House in Unequal Shares

If each member of a group or couple purchasing a home together can put up the same amount of money for the down payment, pay equal shares of the mortgage and other expenses, and will contribute equally to any necessary labor for fixing the place up, it seems self-evident that each person should have an equal share of the owner-ship. However, it is common that this kind of absolute equality does not exist. Often one person will for some reason have more money for the required down payment. It is also common that one person can afford a larger monthly payment than the other, or that one has skills (e.g., carpentry) and can renovate a home while the other can only sit by, beer in hand, and kibitz.

In this section, we discuss some factors to consider in determining whether, or how, to own a home in unequal shares along with some suggestions about completing the necessary paperwork. You will notice that some factors are easy to express in terms of cash (which makes comparison easy) while others are nearly impossible to evaluate. For example, work can be equated to cash by determining a fair hourly wage and then multiplying it by the number of hours worked. But what value do you assign to someone's ability to borrow the down payment from his parents — especially in a society structured to reward the owners of capital? Of course, we don't mean to sug-gest that you must always arrive at a mathematically exact determination of fairness — as you'll see, we suggest that it's enough to decide on a rough equity that satisfies both of you. Let's look at some typical situations:

**a) Unequal Owernship at the Start Turns into Equal Ownership Later:** For our next example, let us fantasize that we are drawing up a contract for Gertrude and Adam. Gertrude can come up with the full $15,000 required for the down payment for a little cottage with a mansard roof. Adam can pay only one-half the monthly mortgage costs, insurance, and maintenance. The two eventually want to own the home equally but also want a fair way to account for Gertrude's down payment. Gertrude could have made a gift of one-half of the down payment to Adam, but she didn't feel quite that generous. Here is an alternative plan. We would suggest that Gertrude call one-half of her down payment a *loan* to Adam that either could be paid back in monthly installments or deferred until the house is sold. To tidy up this arrangement, the two should complete a contract. This contract would record the couple's 50-50 ownership interest, since each one has now put up equal payment. They should, of course, execute a note so that they will have a record of the loan.

---

### Promissory Note for Down Payment

I, Adam acknowledge receipt of a loan of $7,500 from Gertrude, to be used as my share of the down payment for our house located at 10 Rufus St., Pittsburg, PA. I agree to pay this sum back, plus interest, at the rate of 10% per annum, by making monthly payments of $_____. If this loan and all interest due has not been repaid by the time the house is sold, the remaining balance owed shall be paid to Gertrude before Adam receives any proceeds from that sale.

Dated: _____     Signature: _____
                                              Adam
Dated: _____     Signature: _____
                                              Gertrude

---

**b) 2/3–1/3 Down Payment; 2/3–1/3 Monthly Payments = 2/3-1/3 Ownership:** Tina and Bob decide to purchase a home. Tina has more capital than Bob so they decide that Tina will make two-thirds of the down payment and own two-thirds of the house. To keep things simple, it is decided that Tina will also pay two-thirds of the mortgage, taxes, and insurance.

Here's the contract they drew up.

---

### Contract with Ownership and Payments Split 2/3-1/3

We, Tina Foote and Bob Bibbige enter into this contract and agree as follows:

1. *Property:* We agree to purchase the house known as 451 Morton Street, in Upper Montclair, New Jersey.

2. *Contributions:* We agree to contribute the following money for this purchase:

Tina Foote                    $20,000.00
Bob Bibbiage                  $10,000.00

3. *Ownership:* We shall own the property as tenants-in-common, and shall own the property as follows:

| | |
|---|---|
| Tina F. | 2/3 |
| Bob B. | 1/3 |

4. *Expenses and Mortgage:* We agree that all expenses, including mortgage, taxes, insurance, and repairs on the house, will be paid as follows:

| | |
|---|---|
| Tina F. | 2/3 |
| Bob B. | 1/3 |

At the time of sale, the initial contributions (Tina $20,000, Bob $10,000) will first be paid back, and the remainder will be divided two-thirds to Tina and one-third to Bob.

5. *Contingencies:*

a) In the event that either of us decides to leave the house, the other has the option to sell the house or to purchase the other's share at net fair market value. This is to be done within six months from receipt of a written request to sell or be bought out. If the one that remains wants to purchase the other's share, she will get that share appraised and shall purchase it at the net fair market value if the other agrees. If the other disagrees with this appraised market value, he/she may also choose an appraiser, with the two appraisers themselves choosing a third opinion. The three appraisers will meet and jointly arrive at the fair market value of the share. Any appraisers fees will be paid equally by Bob and Tina.

b) In the event that we decide to separate and both want to keep the house, we shall try to reach a satisfactory agreement. If by the end of two weeks we cannot, then we shall ask a friend to flip a coin. The winner of the toss has the right to purchase the house from the other provided he/she pays the fair market value of the other's share within 90 days, the fair market value will be arrived at under the terms of clause 5(a) of this agreement.

c) In the event of the death of one of us, the other has the right to purchase that share from this estate within six months. The value of the share is to be determined as set our above.

6. *Binding:* This agreement shall be binding on both of us and our respective heirs, executors, administrators, successors, and assigns.

In witness, we have executed this agreement on the date given.

Signed in _____     _____
(City)                                        (State)

Dated: _____     Signature: _____
                                                 Tina Foote

Dated: _____     Signature: _____
                                                 Bob Bibbage

(Notarization is necessary if you wish to record this agreement.)

**c) Another Case Where One Person Invests More Money in the House than the Other at the Start:** It is common that one person has more money to invest than the other, but they want to own the house equally eventually. Suppose, for example, that Jeannie has just inherited $30,000 and can make the entire down payment, while Joe either has no money or only a small amount for the down payment, but does have a steady job and can pay his share (or more than his share) of the monthly payments. In addition, let's assume that the house is an older one in need of lots of repairs and that Joe is a professional carpenter. Jeannie and Joe can take title to the house as "tenants in common" and at the same time can sign a separate contract which makes it clear that they own the house in proportion to the dollar amounts that each has contributed. The contract is then recorded at the County Recorder's office in the county where the property is located. Here is a detailed example of how this sort of agreement might read. Of course, the specifics of your agreement will differ. When houses are owned in unequal shares title should be taken as "tenants in common."

---

## AGREEMENT

Jeannie Parker and Joe Richards agree as follows:

1) That Jeannie and Joe will purchase the house at 1639 Carolina St., Salem, Oregon. Their initial investment (down payment and closing costs) will be $30,000, of which Jeannie will contribute $28,000 and Joe, $2,000. Title to the house will be recorded as "Jeannie Parker and Joe Richards as Tenants in Common."

2) Joe and Jeannie will each make one-half of the monthly mortgage, tax and homeowners insurance payments.

3) Joe will contribute labor and materials to improve the house. His labor will be valued at $12.00 per hour and the materials will be valued at their actual cost.

4) A notebook (or computer disk) entitled "Exhibit A-'Homeowners Record' for 1639 Carolina Street" will be maintained and is hereby incorporated into, and made a part of, this contract as Exhibit A. Joe and Jeannie shall record the following information in their "Homeowners Record."*

    a) The $28,000 initial contribution made to purchase the house by Jeannie;
    b) The $2,000 initial contribution made to purchase the house by Joe;
    c) All money Jeannie contributes for house payments, real property taxes and homeowners insurance;
    d) Joe's labor on home improvements valued at $12.00 per hour;
    e) The dollar amount that Joe pays for supplies and materials necessary for home improvements;

---

* The system we set out here is simple and reasonably fair. It credits both parties with all contributions made (not only those which go to equity). It allocates any natural increase in the value of the home along the lines of total contribution and ignores the fact that Jeannie made a large portion of her contribution before Joe. If you want to work out a more exactly accurate (and complicated) system, see a computer. Several of our friends are using this sort of system and find that it works well.

110

f) All money that Joe contributes for house payments, real property taxes and homeowners insurance.

5) The proportion of the house owned by Jeannie and Joe respectively as of any particular date shall be computed as follows:

a) The total dollar amount of the contributions by both Joe and Jeannie as set out in paragraph 4 shall be separately totaled;

b) The total net equity interest in the house shall be computed by subtracting the amount of all mortgages and encumbrances as well as reasonable costs of sale to a third party from the fair market value of the house as of the date the computation is made. If Joe and Jeannie can't agree on the fair market value, they shall have the house appraised. This shall be done by each of them designating a licensed real estate broker or salesperson who is familiar with the neighborhood to do an appraisal. These two appraisers shall choose a third real estate salesperson or broker who shall also make an appraisal. The average of the three appraisals will be the fair market value of the house;

c) The smaller total arrived at in Section 5a of this contract shall be placed above the total amount invested by both people to form a fraction. This fraction represents the share of the total joint net equity interest in the house owned by the person with the smaller share. The remainder of the total joint net equity interest belongs to the person with the larger share.

*EXAMPLE: If after living together for five years, Joe's contributions totals $20,000 and Jeannie's $40,000, Joe would be entitled to $\frac{20,000}{60,000}$ or 1/3 of the value of the total equity in the house. Assuming that the fair market value of the house was $150,000 and all mortgages and other encumbrances total $60,000, this would mean that Joe would be entitled to 1/3 of $90,000 or $30,000.*

6) Either Joe or Jeannie can terminate this agreement at any time. If this occurs, it is understood that the person with the larger equity interest in the house as computed under the terms of paragraph 5 above shall have first choice as to whether he or she wishes to stay living in the house.

7) Should separation occur and a decision made under the terms of paragraph 6 of this contract concerning who is to stay in the house, the person leaving is entitled to receive at least one-half of his or her share as computed under paragraph 5 of this contract in cash within ninety days of the decision to separate. In addition, the person staying shall give the person leaving a three-year mortgage for the remaining portion of his or her share not paid in cash. Said mortgage will be recorded at the County Recorder's office and is payable in 36 equal monthly installments at 9% interest. If the person who wishes to stay in the house is unable to meet the terms of this paragraph, the house shall be sold and the proceeds divided according to the shares established under paragraph 5a of this contract.

8) This agreement should be binding on our respective heirs, executors, administrators and assigns. ·

| Date | Joe Richards |
|------|--------------|

| Date | Jeannie Parker |
|------|----------------|

(Notarization is necessary if you wish to record.)

## 5. If One Person Moves Into A House Already Owned By The Other, What Legal Steps Can Be Taken To Protect Both Parties?

We are commonly asked questions by unmarried couples trying to figure out how to deal with the thicket of legal, practical and emotional problems that can pop up when one person moves into another's house. Sometimes it seems that even the most relaxed people have problems when one invades another's turf. Let's look at a typical situation. A friend (let's call him Alan) calls to say that he has just moved in with his lover (Faye) and that they plan to live in her house. Faye has asked Alan to share equally the monthly house payments, real property taxes, fire insurance, etc. Alan's response to this request is to say, "OK, but only if I somehow get to own part of the house."

As it turns out, the house Fay lives in is worth about $150,000, the existing mortgage is $100,000, and her net equity is slightly less than $50,000 (remember to arrive at net equity you have to subtract costs of sale). Fay agrees with Alan that if he pays one-half of the payments, he should get some interest in the house, but she raises two good points. The first is that, since she already has a big investment in the house, Alan couldn't hope to get much of a share by paying one-half of the monthly payments. Her second point is in the form of a question. Assuming that it was decided to give Alan an equity (ownership) interest in the house, how could it be fairly done? All of this was getting a little hard to work out over the phone, so we invited Alan and Faye over for a pot of tea and a discussion of possible solutions to their problem. Here are several:

a) The simplest solution would be for Alan to forget buying a share of the house and have him pay Faye a monthly amount for rent. Of course, we pointed out to Faye that this should in fairness be considerably less than the one-half of mortgage, tax and insurance costs that she first requested. Why? Because Faye is buying the house and Alan is not. We suggest that if this approach were adopted, Faye and Alan should check the amounts paid by other people sharing houses in their neighborhood to arrive at a fair rent;

b) Another simple solution would be for Alan to pay Faye an amount equal to one-half of the value of her net equity in exchange for her deeding the house to both of

112

them either as "joint tenants" or "tenants in common." In this situation as the net equity is about $22,000, this would mean that Alan would need to pay Faye $11,000. We explained to Alan and Faye that if they followed this approach, they would probably want to make a contract to deal with questions such as who keeps the house if they break up, etc. (see D1-4 of this chapter). But before we could get too far with this discussion, Alan ended it by standing up and turning his pockets inside out. He had eight dollars and a Swiss army knife with a broken can opener. Even in these days of easy credit this didn't seem to be quite enough for a down payment.

c) A third possible way to resolve Alan and Faye's problem is less simple. Alan and Faye could sign a contract under which Alan agrees to pay one-half (or all or any other fraction) of the monthly expenses in exchange for a percentage of the total equity equal to the proportion his payments bear to the total amount of money invested in the house by both parties.* After we all talked for a while, it became clear that Alan and Faye wished to work out a variation of this approach. As Alan said, "I want to think of myself as more than a boarder, but I don't have the cash to pay for one-half of Faye's share." Here is what they worked out.

---

### 57 Primrose Path Contract

Alan Martineau and Faye Salinger agree as follows:

1) That Faye owns the house at 57 Primrose Path, Omaha, Nebraska, subject to a mortgage with the Prairie National Bank in the amount of $100,000;

2) That Alan and Faye agree that the house has a fair market value of $150,000 as of the date this contract is signed and that Faye's net equity interest (after costs of sale) is $40,000;

3) That commencing on the date that this contract is signed, Alan shall pay all monthly expenses for property taxes, homeowners insurance, mortgage payments and necessary repairs and shall continue to do so until his total payments equal $75,000 or until the parties separate;

4) When Alan makes payments in the amount of $75,000 as set out in paragraph 3, Faye shall deed the house to "Faye Salinger and Alan Martineau as Tenants in Common."** From this date on, the house shall be owned equally by Alan and Faye and all expenses for taxes, mortgage insurance and repairs shall be shared equally;

5) Should Alan and Faye separate prior to the time that Alan contributes $75,000, the house shall continue to belong to Faye and Alan will be required to leave within

---

* People who have read this chapter carefully will realize that this is similar to the approach that Keija and Felix chose in slightly different circumstances. See D4 above.
** Alan and Faye could have chosen "joint tenancy", but after talking the situation over, both decided that tenancy in common fit their needs better. See Section C of this chapter.

thirty days of the decision to separate, but Alan shall be entitled to his share of the equity (see paragraph 7). Alan's share of the total net equity value of the house shall be figured at the rate of one-half of one percent for every month that he pays all of the expenses as set out in paragraph 3 above. For example, if Alan pays all the expenses for two years, his interest in the house equity shall be 12%;

6) Once Alan contributes $75,000 and becomes a "tenant in common" with Faye, he shall have an equal opportunity to stay in the house if a separation occurs. If the couple cannot agree amicably who is to stay and who to go after they become "tenants in common," they shall have a friend flip a coin with the winner getting to purchase the share of the other and remain in the house;

7) If a separation occurs either before or after Alan becomes a "tenant in common," the person leaving shall be entitled to receive his or her share of the net equity within ninety days of moving out. If there is a dispute about the fair market value of the house, Faye and Alan shall each select a licensed real estate person to make an appraisal. These two people shall themselves select a third licensed real estate person to make a third appraisal. The three appraisals shall be averaged to determine the fair market value. If it proves impossible for the person who wins the coin flip to pay off the person leaving within ninety days, the other person (the coin flip loser) shall have an additional ninety days to raise the cash to buy out the other person. If neither person is willing or able to buy out the other, the house shall be sold and the proceeds divided under the terms of this agreement.

| | |
|---|---|
| Date | Faye Salinger |
| Date | Alan Martineau |

**NOTE:** Several people have asked us how Alan and Faye decided that Alan should pay $75,000 for a one-half interest in the house and how they decided that he should get credit for one-half of one percent of the net equity for every month that he paid all of the expenses. As we didn't know for sure, we asked them. Here is Faye's reply:

"We were interested in approximate fairness—not absolute statistical accuracy even if that were possible. We figured that as I already had $40,000 in the house after costs of sale were subtracted and that the house was likely to go up in value, it would be fair to require that Alan contribute more as his payments would be made gradually. Also, I wanted to give up my full-time job and have more time for painting Japanese miniatures, so I was anxious to have Alan pay all the expenses—taxes, repairs, insurance as well as mortgage payments. $75,000 seemed to be an amount that we could both live with. We gave Alan credit for all of his expenses as part of buying the house—not just his mortgage payments, because we felt that this worked out fairly for us. To arrive at the one-half of one percent per month (or 6% per year) figure, we did some arithmetic and concluded that it would take Alan about eight years (60 months) to contribute his $75,000 and become a one-half owner. If you divide 50% by eight years, you come out to 6% per year or one-half of one percent per month. I am aware that Alan is getting a pretty good deal, but so am I as I don't have to worry about any house expenses for eight years."

A fourth way to handle this problem would be for Faye to sell Alan one-half of the house at present fair market value, and take a note for the payment. The note would have to be paid in full if the house were to be sold or re-financed. This method would be very generous to Alan because he would be getting the advantage of ownership (meaning tax advantages and increases due primarily to inflation) with no money down. If Alan and Faye had taken this approach their agreement should look like this:

We, Faye S. and Alan M. agree as follows:

1) Faye now owns the house at 57 Primrose Path, Omaha, Nebraska, subject to a mortgage for $100,000.

2) The present value of the home is agreed to be $150,000.

3) Faye hereby sells one-half of the home to Alan for $75,000 and retains a one-half interest in the house (also valued at $75,000).

4) The $75,000 will be paid by Alan as follows:

$50,00: Alan agrees to assume one-half of the $100,000 mortgage and to pay one-half of the monthly mortgage payments.

$25,000: Alan will sign a note to Faye for the sum of $25,000 plus interest at 10 percent per annum to be paid in full when the house is sold.

(You could also include any payment schedule you desire, and the note can be secured by the property if you desire.)

5) All other costs of the home, including taxes, and insurance, and utilities, will be divided evenly.

6) At the time of sale of the property, after all other costs, Faye will first receive the payment on Alan's note plus the interest due, and the remaining profit (or loss) will be divided evenly between Alan and Faye.

(You may add other clauses you want, including "in case of separation" provisions, arbitration clauses, etc.)

Dated: _____     Signature: _____
                                                     Faye S.

Dated: _____     Signature: _____
                                                     Alan M.

**A NOTE ON TAXES:** It is important to keep in mind tax consequences when selling a share of a home. If you receive no money for the sale in a particular year, there is no taxable gain, or income, from the sale. If you do receive money from the sale, you have to determine what percentage was return on your initial capital (not taxed), what percent was interest on the note (taxed as ordinary income), and what percentage was profit on the sale (treated as capital gain, if you had owned the home for more than a year). It makes good sense to spend an hour with an accountant whenever you are putting together a house deal, unless you have thoroughly familiarized yourself with all tax implications.

# tarting a Family

One evening you dream about little feet scampering about your house. After satisfying yourself that it's not a dog, cat or hamster that you are hankering for, you and your mate decide that, even though you are not interested in getting married, you would like to have a child. While there are no insurmountable legal problems involved in having children without being married, there are a few things you will want to think about.*

## A. DECIDING TO HAVE A CHILD (OR ABORTION)

A father recently came to us and asked if he had to support his child in the following circumstances. He and his mate decided not to have children when they commenced living together. After a couple of years they got married and again rejected the idea of having children. They lived together for two years after the marriage, and both continued to agree that they didn't want children. They then decided to separate. A day or two before they parted, the woman (by her own admission) ceased using her diaphragm without telling the man, in an attempt to get pregnant. She succeeded, although the fact that she was pregnant wasn't known until six weeks after the separation. **Yes,** the father does have a duty to support.

Courts are not interested in why people have children. Whether you decide to have children only after signing a contract, or by throwing the I Ching, or checking the location of the planets, or just letting it happen is legally irrelevant. If a child arrives,

---

* We are talking about having children naturally. The problems unmarried persons encounter adopting children within the United States can be insurmountable. If you wish to adopt, you may well find yourself getting married for this purpose. Although some states such as California now allow single parent adoption in some circumstances, if the single person is living with someone or if both members of an unmarried couple want to adopt, it is unlikely the state would approve such an adoption. Some unmarried couples are able to adopt children in foreign countries, particularly if the country is poor and has a large number of orphans. An exception to this rule occurs when you want to adopt a child who is already living with you. If you have been caring for the child for a long time and the natural parents are out of the picture or approve the adoption, your adoption petition will probably be granted, especially if you are related to the child.

both parents have a duty to support. It makes no difference whatsoever whether the parents are or are not married. But is this fair to the man in the above situation? Perhaps not, but we aren't writing a book about fairness, only about the law the way it is.

What about abortion? That's simple. A woman who is pregnant can get an abortion without the consent of the father, whether or not she is married. According to the United States Supreme Court case *Roe v. Wade*, 410 U.S. 133 (1973), an adult woman's decision can be regulated by the state only in the following manner:*

1. Prior to the end of the first trimester (3 months) of pregnancy, the state may not interfere with or regulate the physician's decision, reached in consultation with his patient, that the pregnancy should be terminated.

2. From the end of the first trimester (3 months) of pregnancy until the fetus becomes viable (is capable of living outside the mother), the state may regulate the abortion procedure only to the extent that such regulation relates to the preservation and protection of the health of the mother.

3. After the fetus becomes viable, the state may prohibit abortion altogether, except in those cases necessary to preserve the life or health of the mother.

4. The state may declare abortions performed by persons other than physicians licensed by the state to be unlawful.

The practical aspects of this case for a woman are that, if you suspect you are pregnant and want an abortion, you should contact a physician as early as possible for verification, and you should compare prices before you select the physician or clinic that will perform the abortion.   The practical aspect for a man is that there is legally nothing he can do to influence a woman's decision to have or not to have a baby. This is true even if they are married and he desperately wants the child.

What about "Right To Life" groups and their fight to pass a constitutional amendment banning abortion? We are against it. While abortion makes us as queasy as the next person, we believe that a woman must have the legal freedom to make the choice. We have seen too many seventeen-year olds, pregnant and miserable, for whom motherhood would be a disaster, to think otherwise. Passage of a constitutional amendment banning abortion will simply drive tens of thousands of women out of hospitals and back to the rusty knives of the side-alley butchers. Of course, no woman should be coerced through the welfare or prison system, or in any other way, to have an abortion that she doesn't want, but at the same time no one should be required to have a child to salve someone else's conscience.

---

* Do minors also have the right to abortion? They do, but it is not as absolute as the right of adult women. The Supreme Court has invalidated laws requiring parental consent for minors' abortions. *Planned Parenthood of Missouri v. Danforth*, 428 U.S. 52 (1976), *Bellotti v. Baird*, 443 U.S. 622. However, in M.L. v. Matheson, 101 S.Ct. 1164, (1981) the Supreme Court upheld a Utah statute requiring parental **notification** before a minors' abortion. As things stand now, parental consent cannot be required, but unemancipated minors may have to contend with parental notification if they live in a state that has a law like Utah's.

What about the rights of the father? Doesn't it seem somehow unfair to leave all the decision-making to the mother? If she decides to have the child, he has the legal obligation to support it, but if she wants an abortion, he has nothing to say. Yes, this is unfair and for that reason may not last. We expect legislation to be introduced, once the "Right To Life" people fail to pass their constitutional amendment, giving a father equal rights with the mother in deciding whether or not to get an abortion if the couple has agreed in advance by contract to share this decision — unless, of course, the mother's health is threatened, in which case she would have sole power to terminate the pregnancy. If the legal responsibilities of parents to care for and support their children are to survive in anything like the form in which we know them, both parents must have a say in deciding when to, and when not to, have children.

## B. NAMING THE BABY

In the great majority of states you may give your child any name you like. This includes first, middle and last names. You do not have to give the baby the last name of either father or mother. Thus Mary Jones and Jack Smith could name their child Ephraim Moonbeam if it pleased them. There are a few states that have laws which require the child of a woman who is married at the child's birth to bear the father's surname—but these laws are being challenged and are not widespread.*

In most states the normal procedure for naming a baby is substantially as follows: While in the hospital a representative (frequently a volunteer) of the Health Department or similar agency asks the new mother what the child's name is, plus some other questions regarding the health of the mother and the occupation of the father. This information is then typed on a form that the mother is requested to sign. The mother **does not** have to give the child a name at this time, and she does not have to identify the father, although there may be some pressure to do so. The birth will be registered in any case. In some states a birth certificate reveals whether or not the parents are married. In most states, the birth certificate does not reveal this information.

If the baby was not born in a medical facility, the mother and/or person officiating at the birth are legally obligated to notify state or county health officials of the birth. Again, there is no requirement to name the baby at this time although it is common to do so. If the mother later decides on a name for the child or decides to give the information regarding the father, she should contact the appropriate state agency which usually has a name such as the Department of Vital Statistics, which will furnish her with a form to fill out to amend the birth certificate.

**CAUTION:** It is a terrible idea to list a person as the natural father if that person is not, in fact, the father. Many women are tempted to do this, especially if they no longer see the natural father and are now involved with someone else. Please be realistic and realize that your new relationship may not last forever, and you may later regret the

---

* South Carolina requires that an illegitimate child legitimated by marriage take the husband's name. S.C. 20-170.

naming of the wrong person.* We have seen many cases involving complicated questions of paternity and support grow from the seemingly simple act of listing the wrong person as the father of a child. Once a person is listed as a father, it is very difficult, and sometimes impossible, for the mother or the child to get the state to de-list him.

On the other hand, if you feel you have been wrongly named as a father on a birth certificate, this is not proof to a court that you are the father. In a paternity action or a support action you would still be able to contest paternity. The state will not take your name off a birth certificate simply because you state you are not the father, but an attorney may be able to assist you in bringing legal action to have your name removed, if you act promptly. Recent advances in blood chemistry research make it possible to determine paternity (and the lack thereof) with considerable accuracy.

## C. PATERNITY

Very simply, paternity means "the state of being a father". For the reasons outlined in Sections C, D, E, F, and G of this chapter, it is essential that the natural father sign a paper stating that he is the father as soon as possible after the baby is born.** This is for the protection of the mother, the baby, and especially the father. Mix-ups over paternity are complicated, humiliating and often expensive. As you will see from reading the rest of this chapter, the law in the legitimacy-illegitimacy-paternity area is so confused that it's hard to be sure what a father's rights are unless he signs a

---

* For further information on naming a baby and changing names and/or amending a birth certificate, see *How To Change Your Name* (California edition) by David Loeb (coupon at end of book).
** What happens if the father doesn't sign the paternity statement when the child is born, but waits and signs it later? This is OK if he signs it before any dispute over custody, adoption, etc. develops. However, if he waits until a custody fight develops and then tries to improve his legal position by legitimating his child, many courts will say that it is too late. If you are in this position, see a lawyer and refer to *In re L.A.H.*, an Alaska decision which allowed a natural father to legitimate his child after an adoption petition was filed (5 FLR 2718)

paternity statement. You can prepare the necessary form yourself quite easily by reference to the sample shown below. Please do not let your excitement over the baby allow you to forget this simple detail. We include here two sample paternity statements. The first is the traditional type signed only by the father. The second is designed to be signed by both parents. We introduce this second form because we have recently encountered several cases where, after a man has signed the first type statement, the mother, wanting to frustrate his custody and visitation rights, has denied that he, in fact, was the father.

**SAMPLE 1**

---

### ACKNOWLEDGEMENT OF PATERNITY

Lazarus Sandling hereby acknowledges that he is the natural father of Clementine Conlon Sandling, born January 1, 19    to Rebecca Conlon in New York City, New York.*

Lazarus Sandling further states that he has welcomed Clementine Conlon Sandling into his home and that it is his intention and belief that he has taken all steps necessary to fully legitimate Clementine Conlon Sandling for all purposes, including the right to inherit from, and through him, at the time of his death.

Lazarus Sandling further expressly acknowledges his duty to properly raise and adequately support Clementine Conlon Sandling.


---------------------------------                    ---------------------------------
Date                                                 Lazarus Sandling

                                    Notarize

---

**SAMPLE 2**

---

### ACKNOWLEDGEMENT OF PARENTHOOD

Lazarus Sandling and Rebecca Conlon hereby acknowledge that they are the natural parents of Clementine Conlon Sandling, born January 1, 19    in New York City, New York.

---

* As noted above, there is no legal reason why Clementine's last name must be Sandling for purposes of legitimation. However, as a practical matter our society takes this sort of tradition seriously and it may be easier for everyone in years to come if the child has Lazarus' last name, or a hyphenated version of Lazarus' and Rebecca's names.

Lazarus Sandling and Rebecca Conlon further state that they have welcomed Clementine Conlon Sandling into their home and that it is their intention and belief that Clementine is fully legitimated for all purposes, including the right to inherit from and through Lazarus Sandling.*

Lazarus Sandling and Rebecca Conlon further expressly acknowledge their legal responsibility to properly raise and adequately support Clementine Conlon Sandling.

_____          _____
Date                                          Rebecca Conlon


_____          _____
Date                                          Lazarus Sandling


Notarize

---

**(Tear-out Paternity Statements can be found in the Appendix)**

**FORM PREPARATION NOTE:** Your paternity statement should be prepared in triplicate and signed in front of a notary who will then stamp each document. Notarization is not strictly required, but it is a good idea. In the event of the death of the father, the paternity statement will have to be presented to various bureaucracies such as Social Security. The notary stamp proves that the signature is legitimate and that the document wasn't forged after death occurred. The mother and father should each keep one copy and the third copy should be kept safe for the child. Some states are setting up procedures for filing paternity statements with the state Bureau of Vital Statistics. It would be wise for you to do this if possible.


## D. LEGITIMACY

Most states and the federal government are moving away from the old concepts of "legitimacy" and "illegitimacy". And about time too — there is something weird about a society that places a higher value on children whose parents happened to get married before doing what comes naturally. A number of states such as California have

---

* There is never a legal problem of a child of unmarried parents inheriting from its mother, but in the past there have been problems inheriting from a father in some states. See Section J of this chapter.

adopted the Uniform Parentage Act*which says that "the parent and child relationship extends equally to every child and to every parent, regardless of the marital status of the parents". **But even in states where concepts of "legitimacy" and "illegitimacy" are mostly out the window, it is still legally important to know who a child's natural parents are. In inheritance, child support, custody, adoption, and many other areas of the law, the rights and duties of parents are clearly marked out. If a father does not voluntarily sign a paternity agreement as discussed above, the state will try to establish that he is the father in other ways.** In states that have adopted the Uniform Parentage Act a man is presumed to be the father if:

**Circumstance 1:** He is married to the mother at the time the child is born, or was married to her within 300 days of the birth of the child. This means that, if the man dies or there is an annulment or divorce while the mother is pregnant, he is still presumed to be the father.

**Circumstance 2:** He and the mother, before the birth of the child, attempted to get married in the sense that they got a license, had a ceremony, etc., even though the marriage wasn't valid for some reason such as one of the partners still being married to someone else.

and

The child was born during the attempted marriage or within 300 days after its termination, whether by court order, death or simple separation.

**Circumstance 3:** After the child's birth he and the natural mother have married (or gone through a ceremony in apparent compliance with law) although the marriage could later be annulled for some reason;

and

a) With his consent, he is named the child's father on the birth certificate, or

b) He is obliged to support the child under a written, voluntary promise, or by court order. (This is the paternity statement situation.)

**Circumstance 4:** He receives the child into his home and openly holds out the child as his natural child.

You will note if you re-read these rules that we are dealing with presumptions. This normally means in law that a certain fact situation will be presumed to produce a certain legal conclusion unless rebutted by stronger evidence.** As we saw just above, if a man takes a child into his home and says that he is the father even though he was never married to the child's mother, he is legally presumed to be the father. This doesn't mean that he **is** the father — he might still be able to rebut the presumption, that is, prove that, even though he received a child into his home and told his friends

---

* The Uniform Parentage Act has been adopted in California, Colorado, Hawaii, Minnesota, Montana, North Dakota, Washington and Wyoming.
** Some states have had a conclusive presumption (one that can't be rebutted) that says that a child born to a married couple who were living together at the time of conception belongs to the husband unless he was sterile or impotent. These laws are being changed in the face of new types of blood tests which are extremely accurate in determining paternity.

and family that he was the father, in fact, he was not. This is where court fights, blood tests, etc. are common.

Unfortunately, many states have not followed California's example and adopted the Uniform Parentage Act. They still use the terms "legitimate" and "illegitimate". However, in a long line of judicial decisions extending from *Levy v. Louisiana*, 391 U.S. 68 (1968) to *Trimble v. Gordon*, 430 U.S. 762 (1977), the United States Supreme Court has regularly been striking down state laws that give legitimate children more rights than illegitimate children. Thus, even in states that make these distinctions, they mean less than they used to.

In states that still label children, it is normally possible to change the label from illegitimate to legitimate as follows:*

⚫ By the natural parents later marrying each other;

*or*

⚫ By the father signing a paternity statement — that is, acknowledging that the child is his in writing.

⚫ Some states also would hold that "legitimation" occurs if the father welcomes the child into his home and/or holds himself out to be the father.

⚫ By going to court and having a judge make a ruling. In many states such as New York this can be done by both parents petitioning the court together in a non-adversary proceeding.

If children are born during a marriage that is later annulled, most states have laws that preserve the legitimacy of the children. And remember, the legitimacy of a child is only relevant as to the child's relationship with the father, and the father's family, and the father's benefactors. The mother's relationship with her child is not changed by the child's status.

**SUMMARY**: If you re-read this section and the previous one, you should conclude that signing a paternity statement is the best (and sometimes the only) way to be sure that your child is legitimate. If you do this, you need not worry about understanding the other legal technicalities.

## E. PLANNING FOR SEPARATION

Most parents plan to stay together at least until their children are grown. But somehow the glue that held families together in former generations seems to have lost much of its stick. Whether married or living together, many parents find themselves separating and facing the task ot raising their children while living apart. Doing this in a constructive, humane way is a great challenge. It requires both parents to submerge

---

* You can find out your state law by checking your state legal code. Look in the index under the heading "Children" and the sub-heading "Legitimate". If you have trouble, ask the librarian to help you. In a few states you will find that in theory it is almost impossible to legitimate a child. These laws are no longer constitutional because in *Trimble v. Gordon*, 430 U.S. 762 (1977) the Supreme Court ruled that, while states may set up differing standards as to what proof is necessary to establish paternity, they can't be completely arbitrary. Thus, the court apparently ruled that formal acknowledgment of paternity by the father **or** an adjudication of paternity by a court are always sufficient to establish paternity of a child and allow the child to be treated as if he or she were legitimate.    However, in a subsequent decision, *Lalli v. Lalli*, 99 S. Ct. 518 (1978), the Supreme Court ruled that a New York law which only allows legitimation by court action and not by a paternity statement is valid at least as far as inheritance is concerned where there is no will. This is a very confusing case involving five separate opinions by the nine justices. Our conclusion is that a paternity statement is still of some value in New York but that parents may wish to consider formal court action and certainly should prepare a will.

their egos in the best interests of the child(ren). Since unmarried couples don't get divorces, they have no automatic occasion to involve judges and lawyers in their child-raising responsibilities. They are free to make their own child custody, support and visitation arrangements. We believe that, if possible, it is best that they do so.

Here we give you three sample written agreements that you may find helpful. They are quite different, ranging from a joint support-joint custody agreement to a more traditional dad supports-mom takes care of the children arrangement. You may find that no one of these agreements fits your situation perfectly and that you will want to use elements of all three. Remember, no agreement concerning custody, support or visitation can ever be permanently binding, even those ordered by a judge. Because circumstances change, it is necessary that parents approach their agreements with a spirit of openness. What is a fair amount of support today will probably not be enough tomorrow. Custody with one parent may work brilliantly for a period of time and then not so well. Your agreements must be living documents, not museum pieces frozen under glass forever. Think of your first agreement as a mutual statement detailing needs and expectations. You want to lay a solid foundation that will support the changes and additions that will surely come.

**NOTE:** We assume that by this point you have already both signed a statement acknowledging parenthood, or at least the father has signed such a statement. If this has not been done, turn back to Section C of this chapter. It is essential to everyone's interests (most especially the father's) that a paternity statement be signed.

---

### FIRST SAMPLE SEPARATION AGREEMENT

Rebecca Conlon and Lazarus Sandling, having decided to no longer live together make the following agreement for the purpose of raising their child Clementine in a spirit of compromise and cooperation. Both Rebecca and Lazarus agree that they will be guided by the best interests of Clementine and that:

1) Custody of Clementine shall be joint. This means that all major decisions regarding Clementine's physical location, visitation by the non-custodial parent and any other major decisions such as those relating to Clementine's health, education, etc. shall be made jointly. For the first year after this agreement is signed, Lazarus shall take care of Clementine during the day on all working days and Rebecca shall take care of Clementine nights and weekends.

2) At the time this agreement is made, Lazarus' income as a night disc jockey and Rebecca's income as a day horse jockey are approximately equal and neither person shall pay the other child support. Lazarus shall cover Clementine for health and dental insurance at his job and Rebecca shall contribute an equal amount (about $60 per month) for clothes. Each person shall pay routine costs for food and shelter while Clementine is in their custody.

3) If in the future either Lazarus' or Rebecca's income increases to an amount that is more than 30% over what is earned by the other, the person with the higher income

shall be expected to bear a larger share of the child support with the exact amount to be worked out at that time, based on the income of both parents and Clementine's needs.

4) Lazarus and Rebecca will make an effort to remain in the area of New York City where they presently live at least until Clementine is in junior high school.

5) Should Lazarus and Rebecca have trouble agreeing as to visitation, custody, support or any other problem concerning Clementine, they will jointly agree on a program of counseling to attempt to resolve or compromise their differences. Clementine shall be involved in this process to the maximum amount consistent with her age at the time.

_____    _____
Date    Rebecca Conlon

_____    _____
Date    Lazarus Sandling

**NOTE:** If communication between Lazarus and Rebecca completely broke down and one or the other filed a formal custody action in court, this agreement would probably be examined by the judge. But considering the fact that the judge has an independent right to make orders for what he or she considers to be in the "best interests of the child", it probably wouldn't count for too much.

## SECOND SAMPLE SEPARATION AGREEMENT

Sam Matlock and Chris Woodling make this agreement because they have decided to cease living together, but wish to provide for the upbringing and support of their children, Natasha and Jason. Sam and Chris agree as follows:

1) That until Jason and Natasha are both in school (approximately 3 years) Chris shall have primary responsibility for childcare during the week and Sam shall pay child support in the amount of $300 per month per child;

2) That Jason and Natasha shall spend most weekends and at least one month during the summer with Sam and that Sam shall be available for babysitting at least two weekday nights;

3) That all major decisions regarding physical location, support, visitation, education, etc. affecting Jason and Natasha shall be made jointly by Sam and Chris and that Natasha and Jason shall be involved in the decision-making to an extent consistent with their ages at the time;

4) That when both Natasha and Jason are in school, Chris plans to return to her career as a fashion designer at least part-time and that Sam intends to return to school to finish his Ph.D. It is contemplated that during this period of time Chris will earn enough to support the children and Sam will take on a larger share of the childcare duties;

5) Both Sam and Chris are determined to conduct their affairs without recourse to lawyers and courts. If communication becomes difficult, they pledge themselves to participate in a joint program of counseling. If one issue such as physical custody, or amount of support becomes impossible to compromise, they agree that they will submit the dispute to binding arbitration.

_____          _____
Date                                     Sam Matlock

_____          _____
Date                                     Chris Woodling

## THIRD SAMPLE SEPARATION AGREEMENT

Joseph Benner and Josephine Clark agree to live separately from this time on, and,

Joseph Benner and Josephine Clark wish to assure that their children, Nancy Benner, born June 1, 19    , and David Clark, both May 20, 19    , have a secure financial future and receive the necessary support that they will need to lead a safe, happy life. Joseph Benner and Josephine Clark agree to the following:

1. Josephine Clark shall have custody of the above minor children reserving to Joseph Benner liberal rights of visitation, including the right to have the children live with him for two months during the summer.

2. For a period of two years beginning February 1, 198__ Joseph Benner shall pay to Josephine Clark the sum of $700 per month for child support for the two minor children.

3. Josephine Clark shall attempt to find employment. Said employment shall not diminish the amount of child support paid.

4. Beginning February 1, 198__, Joseph Benner shall pay to Josephine Clark the sum of $350 per month for child support of the two minor children. Said support shall continue at the rate of $175 per child per month until each child has reached the age of majority, marries or is otherwise emancipated.

5. All Payments are due on the first day of each month.

6. The provisions of this agreement may be incorporated into any court order in any court action maintained by either party. if any court action is maintained, this agreement shall be presented to the court.

7. This agreement may be modified only by written agreement of both parties or by order of a court.

_____          _____
Date                                      Joseph Benner


_____          _____
Date                                      Josephine Clark

**FORM PREPARATION NOTE:** These agreements should be prepared in duplicate, each party should sign it in front of a notary public, and each party should keep one copy. It is possible to have these agreements made part of a court order but you will probably need an attorney to do this for you. In that you have already done most of the work, you shouldn't be charged an outrageous fee.

## F. CUSTODY

If an unmarried couple breaks up, both parents have an equal right to custody of the child as long as the child has been legitimated. However, if the father has refused to sign a paternity statement or otherwise legitimate his child, he is definitely discriminated against. Why? Because in a series of goofy decisions, the logic of which we can't explain, courts have set up a double standard. A father must support his children, whether legitimate or not, but only has equal rights to custody if he has legitimated them. At the risk of boring you to tears, let us again emphasize the obvious — if a father signs a paternity statement as soon after birth as possible, all this nonsense can be avoided. If he waits until a dispute develops to legitimate his child, it may be too late, but as a general rule even a late legitimation is better than no legitimation as far as a father's rights are concerned.

What do we mean when we say that both parents have equal rights to custody of a legitimate child if they separate? **Just that — unless, or until a judge as part of a custody case makes a different order — neither person has the legal right to deprive the other of the right to have or visit with the children.** If a court does order that one person have custody of the children (say, the mother), if some event such as illness should prevent her from providing care for the child, the other parent (the father) is next in line to exercise custody rights.

**EXAMPLE:** Rebecca Conlon assumes physical custody of Clementine after a break-up with Lazarus Sandling. A year later Rebecca dies or disappears or is injured to the extent that she cannot care for the child. Lazarus, who has signed a paternity statement legitimating Clementine, has the right to custody of the child and any third party seeking custody would have to petition the court and present evidence as to the inability of Lazarus to care properly for Clementine. Now let's change the example and assume that, instead of dropping out of the picture, Rebecca gets married. What are Lazarus' rights? As long as the child has been legitimated, she cannot be adopted by either Rebecca's new husband, or a third party without the consent of Lazarus, unless he had abandoned the child (failed to support or contact the child for a certain length of time). Abandonment has to be proven to the satisfaction of the court.*

**If a child is not legitimate, in most states the father has no legal right to custody if it comes to a fight with the mother, some other relative, or some public agency that wants to place the child in a foster home.** A generation ago, an illegitimate father was treated as if he didn't exist. But in a small step toward sanity, the U.S. Supreme Court ruled in the case of *Stanley v. Illinois*, 405 U.S. 645 (1972) that "The state cannot, consistent with due process requirements, merely presume that unmarried fathers in general and petitioner in particular are unsuitable and neglectful parents ... The denial to unwed fathers of a hearing of fitness accorded to all other parents whose custody of their children is challenged by the state constitutes a denial of equal protection of the laws." The effect of the *Stanley* case has been that illegitimate

---

* Before a parent can be judged to have "abandoned" his or her child, he or she must have failed to visit or support the child for a considerable period of time. In most states this is at least two years, although some have shortened it to one year. If you have no money and thus can't support your child, you can't be viewed legally as abandoning the child as long as you visit regularly.

fathers are now notified and given a right to be heard whenever some legal proceedings affect their children.* In some situations they have been successful in winning custody. BUT—and this is important—fathers of illegitimate children are still discriminated against and still face an uphill battle to win custody. We do not believe that this sort of double standard is consistent with either common sense or the Constitution. Many people believe that eventually the Supreme Court will agree.

## G. VISITATION

The unmarried parent of a legitimate child has the same legal right to visitation that a married parent has (see Section C, Chapter 9). This means that the parent who does not have custody has the right to visit with his or her children at reasonable times. Hopefully visitation, like custody, can be voluntarily worked out to the satisfaction of both parents (see Section F of this chapter), but if this is impossible, a judge will spell it out.

As we noted in the previous sections, the unmarried father of an illegitimate child has the duty to support, but few rights. It is unlikely that a court would order visitation for a father of an illegitimate child.

We are often asked what happens if a non-custodial parent who has disappeared, failed to maintain contact with his or her children, and doesn't provide support suddenly shows up and wants to visit his or her children? Many custodial parents who have established new families fear what they regard as "a ghost from the past". The only answer we can give is that it depends on the circumstances. Judges faced with deciding whether or not to approve visitation in this sort of situation usually start by being suspicious of a new-found desire to visit one's children after years of neglect and are usually attentive to the views of the parent who has performed his or her child-rearing responsibilities. However, if the absent parent is willing to provide support and genuinely demonstrates a desire to establish a solid relationship with the child(ren), the judge will probably allow visitation. Most judges believe that it is healthy for children to have a relationship with both natural parents even if they are less than perfect.

## H. ADOPTIONS

The legitimated child of an unmarried couple cannot be adopted by a third person without the consent of both parents, unless one of the parents has abandoned the child. This means that fathers who sign a paternity statement, support (if they have the ability to do so) and maintain a relationship with their children are in no danger of seeing the children adopted by someone else. Mothers who don't have custody needn't sign a paternity statement, but must help with support if they are able, and visit their children.

The law of most states provides that when a child is "illegitimate", the consent of the natural father is not necessary for his (her) adoption, although the mother and the child depending on its age must consent. Either a state agency or a state-licensed

---

* The U.S. Supreme Court has also ruled that an unwed father (who was closely involved with his child) has the right to veto an adoption if under state law a mother has that right. *Caban v. Mohammed,* 441 U.S. 380 (1979).

adoption agency must submit a report and recommendation in all non-stepparent adoption cases. These agencies have become very cautious recently, and if there is any question as to whether a child has been legitimated, they will withhold their recommendation that an adoption be granted until a court has determined that the father's consent is not necessary, either because the father has forfeited his parental right by abandonment (his failure to support or contact the child during a specified period of time), or because there has been no legitimation. As noted above, recent law changes require that even the father of an illegitimate child be given notice of the adoption court hearing and a chance to be heard.

Stepparent adoption cases are those where one of the natural parents has married someone else, and the new spouse wishes to adopt the children. There is a tendency for these adoptions to be approved more readily than other kinds of adoption, probably because the child is already in the home and will stay there even if the adoption is not approved. However, reports from a governmental (state or county) agency are also required in these cases. This means that the home is visited and a background study is made of the natural parents, the adopting parent and the child. Just as in other kinds of adoptions, whether the child is legitimate or illegitimate will determine whether the natural father must consent to the adoption. The natural mother must always consent unless the court terminates her parental rights by finding she has abandoned the child either through her failure to contact the child or her failure to support the child for a certain length of time.

Now let's look at what might happen given several different fact situations:

**EXAMPLE:** Linda and Frank are not married to each other. Linda has Frank's baby, but Frank takes off before the baby is born and does not contact Linda or the baby and does not send any support. Linda contacts an adoption agency which agrees to arrange for an adoption of the child. Linda must consent to the adoption. Frank's consent is not necessary but an effort must be made to notify him of the proposed adoption. If he shows an interest in the proceedings, he must be given a hearing, but his opposition probably won't be counted for much.

**EXAMPLE:** Same as above, except Linda keeps the baby and later marries Herman. Herman wants to adopt the baby. Linda's consent is necessary but Frank's consent is not. Frank will be notified of the action and is entitled to a hearing if he opposes the adoption.

**EXAMPLE:** Linda and Frank are unmarried. Linda has Frank's baby and they live together several years, then split up and Linda keeps the child. Frank always says that the child is his and continues to visit the child and pay support after he and Linda separate, but never signs a paternity statement. Whether the child can be adopted by either another couple or by Linda's new spouse without the consent of Frank depends on state law. In some states such as California, Frank has legitimated the child by welcoming it into his home and acknowledging that he is the father. This means that in California, if Frank opposes the adoption, he would be able to stop it. However, in other states such as New York, simply living with a child and saying that it is yours is not enough to legitimate it and Frank might be unable to stop an adoption.

**EXAMPLE:** Same as above, except when the baby is born, Frank signs a paternity statement. Linda keeps the child after the split up and later marries Herman, who wishes to adopt the baby. In the meantime, Frank has continued to see and support the child. There is no way that the adoption would be approved in any state without Frank's consent.

**EXAMPLE:** Same as above, except before Linda and Frank split up, Frank has signed a paternity statement legitimating the child. Linda keeps the child, and Frank is never heard from again (or else he visits very seldom and sends no support or very little support for the child). Is Frank's consent to an adoption necessary? Probably. If Frank refuses to consent or can't be found, a court hearing will have to be held to determine whether he has forfeited his parental rights by abandoning the child. Frank will have to be given notice of the hearing and a chance to present his views. If the court finds he has so abandoned the child, the adoption will be allowed.

**EXAMPLE:** Same as above, except when they split up, Frank keeps the child. Linda and Frank must consent to any adoption action and must be notified of any hearing to terminate their parental rights. Of course, if Linda does not support or contact the child for a certain length of time, a court can find that she has abandoned the child and declare that their consent is not necessary.

**NOTE:** Most states provide that a child can be declared "freed for adoption" for reasons other than abandonment. Some of these reasons are imprisonment for a felony, mental retardation, or unfitness of the natural parents. We do not deal specifically with these situations since contested adoption actions are not common in these areas.

## I. SUPPORT OF AN ILLEGITIMATE CHILD

As we noted in Section F, a father has a duty to support even in cases where the child is illegitimate and he has no right to custody. [Both parents have a legal duty to support all their children.] There is no reason for a court to get involved in support questions if the parents can work it out to their mutual satisfaction. In Section D of Chapter 9 we discuss support of legitimate children in detail.

The parent who has custody (most often the mother) or a person acting on behalf of the child can sue the other parent (commonly the father) in a court action and obtain a court order setting an amount of child support the absent parent will have to pay. If the absent parent does not support the child, the District Attorney may prosecute him or her in a criminal action which will result, if he has the ability to support but continues to withhold payment, in his going to jail. The county jails are full of people who failed to take their support obligation seriously.

Of course, if the child is subsequently adopted by another person or persons, all parental rights of the natural parents are terminated and their duty to support the child is also ended. Likewise, if one of the parents should later marry and the new spouse should adopt the child (stepparent adoption), the parent whose parental rights are terminated no longer has a duty to support the child.

## J. BENEFITS FOR THE CHILD OF UNMARRIED PARENTS (SOCIAL SECURITY, ETC.)

There are many benefits that a child can become entitled to through his or her parents. To name a few: Social Security if a parent becomes disabled or dies; union benefits; insurance benefits. Until recently these programs discriminated against illegitimate children — particularly benefits derived through the father. For example, until recently Social Security regulations provided for unequal sharing of benefits among the legitimate and illegitimate children of a deceased or retired or disabled father with a preference for legitimate children. The United States Supreme Court held in the case of *Jimenez v. Weinberger,* 417 U.S. 628 (1974) that this was unconstitutional. Similar discriminating provisions in other government programs have likewise been held to be unconstitutional and now it makes no difference whether a child is legitimate or illegitimate for purposes of receiving Social Security and similar benefits.

As noted earlier in this chapter, we believe strongly in the father signing a paternity statement. If a father dies, benefits under Social Security or other federal, state or private insurance programs may be denied, not because the child is illegitimate, but because there is no proof that the deceased was actually the father. A paternity statement solves this problem.

## K. INHERITANCE RIGHTS OF AN ILLEGITIMATE CHILD

Inheritance laws can be complicated. Most states have provisions that diminish the rights of illegitimate children if a parent dies without leaving a will. Many states provide that an illegitimate child inherits as if he were legitimate from his mother but not from his father, unless, of course, the father has legitimated the child by signing a paternity statement or in some other way sufficient under the law of the state in which the parent lives. In *Trimble v. Gordon,* 430 U. S. 762 (1977) the Supreme Court made it clear that a paternity statement is normally adequate to guarantee the inheritance rights of children born out of wedlock. However, in *Lalli v. Lalli,* 99 S. Ct. 518 (1978) the Court also upheld a New York statute which requires a court decree of paternity (not just a paternity statement) for a child to inherit without a will. We recommend that if you live in a state that has not adopted the Uniform Parentage Act you should play it safe and execute both a will and a paternity statement.

Of course, you can leave your property to anyone you want to in a will, or by other simple trust or joint ownership devices. See Chapter 11.

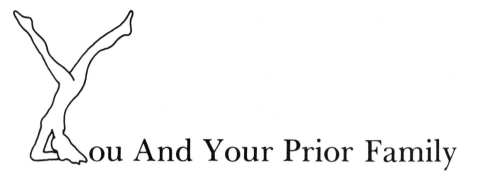

# ou And Your Prior Family

If you have been married previously or are still married to someone other than the person with whom you are living, you might encounter special problems.* This is particularly true when you and a former spouse have left each other in anger and bitterness. Fortunately, more and more people are finding it possible to split up without nasty court battles. We apparently aren't the only ones who have learned that lawyers benefit from domestic strife, and court fights normally last only as long as the money holds out. So try and talk your problems out with your former mate. Remember, you got yourself into the relationship and in the last analysis, you are the only ones who can get yourselves out. It's never too late to try getting along, if not in a loving fashion, at least in a civilized one. Paranoia is almost always a part of separating. If there is nothing major to get upset about, people will manage to worry about who gets the teaspoons or the ten-speed bike. To get on top of this kind of situation, an excellent place to start is with yourself.

## A. GETTING A DIVORCE WHILE LIVING WITH SOMEONE ELSE

### 1. Divorce Based On Fault

A few states still have a divorce system based on "fault". This means that in order to get a divorce one party must prove that the other in some way mistreated him or her. And not only is the person proving fault entitled to a divorce — he or she may also be entitled to a greater share of the couple's property, alimony and custody of the children.

---

* If you live in California, you will find much specific information about custody, visitation, adoption and children of former marriages in *California Marriage and Divorce Law*, by Warner and Ihara. (See order information at the back of this book.)

How do you prove fault? One sure way is to show that a spouse is committing adultery. This means that if you are living with someone and you and your spouse are fighting over kids, alimony, amount of child support or the division of property, you can bet your bottom dollar (if you still have a dollar left) that your living arrangement (adultery) will be dragged into court. How much it will influence a judge's decision is not certain. As the twentieth century marches on, living with someone is not as shocking (even to judges) as it once was, and many will minimize it even in "fault divorce" states, especially those which require the "equitable distribution" of property at divorce. But one thing is sure—it won't count in your favor. If you are employing an attorney to help you with your divorce, it would be wise to discuss your living arrangement with him or her, unless you live in a state which allows a no-fault divorce to be initiated by either spouse without the other's consent.

## CHART 1

## IS DIVORCE ALLOWED ON NO FAULT GROUNDS?

**(This chart is a shorthand guide only. The laws of many states are complicated. Check yours out in detail.)**

### NO-FAULT DIVORCE STATES:*

Most of these states allow no-fault divorce on the petition of either party with no requirement that the parties have lived apart for any particular period of time prior to filing and no right of the other spouse to disagree as to whether incompatibility exists (a few allow a judge to determine if sufficient incompatibility exists for divorce). No-fault states include:

Alabama, Arizona, California, Colorado, Delaware, Florida, Georgia, Indiana, Iowa, Kansas, Kentucky, Maine, Michigan, Minnesota, Montana, Nebraska, New Mexico, North Dakota, Oklahoma, Oregon, Washington and Wyoming.

### MODIFIED NO-FAULT DIVORCE STATES:

Other states allow no-fault divorce only after a certain period of time has passed since separation. In a few of these states, the divorce can be handled on the basis of no-fault only if both spouses agree. Most of these states have retained their fault divorce system with the old grounds for divorce such as adultery for people who don't qualify for a no-fault divorce.

---

* All eight community property states—California, Washington, Arizona, Texas, New Mexico, Nevada, Louisiana and Idaho allow no-fault or modified no-fault divorce. Generally speaking, property acquired in these states after marriage (except by gift or inheritance to one spouse) is community property and divided 50-50 at divorce. In most other states "equitable distribution" laws are used to divide a couple's property acquired after marriage. These laws vary somewhat. If yours is important to you, find out what it ways and how its been interpreted.

Alaska, Arkansas, Connecticut, District of Columbia, Hawaii, Idaho, Louisiana, Maryland, Massachusetts, Mississippi, Missouri, Nevada, New Hampshire, New Jersey, New York, North Carolina, Ohio, Pennsylvania, Rhode Island, South Carolina, Tennessee, Texas, Vermont, Virginia, West Virginia, Utah and Wisconsin.

## FAULT DIVORCE STATES:

The following states allow divorce only after a claim that one person was at fault. Arkansas, Illinois, South Dakota and Utah.

---

**REMEMBER:** Many people get sensible, civilized divorces even in states where there is "fault divorce". They do this by going through the motions of pretending one person is in the wrong when they fill out their court papers, but make their decisions about children, support, and property in a spirit of common sense and compromise rather than "who is more right". If you and your spouse are separating in this spirit (or if you have no property or children to fight about), you need not worry about the effect of living with someone else. But just in case memories grow short, it might make sense to make a written note as to your understanding. Of course, you will have to modify this to fit your circumstances.

---

## CO-OPERATIVE SEPARATION AGREEMENT*

Sean and Barbara Washington agree to the following:

1. That they have decided to go their separate ways and no longer plan to live together.

2. That John Washington, age 5, and Richard Washington, age 3, will reside with Barbara Washington, and Sean will spend as much time as possible with the children.

3. That Sean will provide a reasonable amount of support to Barbara each month, taking into consideration his salary and the needs of the children. Initially, this will be $450 per month.

4. That as neither Sean nor Barbara plan to marry again immediately, it is understood that both will have friendships that may involve sex and may decide to live with someone of the same or the opposite sex.

---

* This sort of agreement is not technically enforceable in court, especially as it relates to the custody of children. As we learn later in this chapter, a court may look at all factors when considering "the best interests of the child". Still, amicable agreement between yourselves is desirable and many judges would give it considerable weight. If one spouse suddenly starts dragging the other's lifestyle into court, a judge might well ask "How come you didn't object to his (her) living with someone the day you signed the 'Separation Agreement', but now suddenly do?"

5. That Sean and Barbara will proceed to get a divorce as amicably as possible and that neither will try to influence the decision of the court by referring to the fact that the other is having a relationship with, or living with, a third person.

| | |
|---|---|
| Date | Barbara Washington |
| Date | Sean Washington |

## 2. "No-Fault Divorce"

Many states (see Chart) have adopted a "no-fault divorce" law. In some of these states such as California even the word "divorce" has been replaced by "dissolution of marriage." The idea behind "no-fault divorce" is simple—a court should not be a place where couples are encouraged to drag each other through a morass of petty wrongs and broken expectations. States that have adopted "no-fault divorce" laws commonly provide that the only grounds for ending a marriage are for such vague reasons as "irretrievable breakdown," "incompatibility of temperament" or "irreconcilable differences." In these states the reasons for the incompatibility are not admissible in court to decide issues of property division, alimony (spousal support), etc. Thus, *whether or not one spouse is living with someone else has no relevancy to the divorce.* However, as we will see in Section B of this chapter, it may be brought up in court in a child custody dispute and as is discussed in Section E below, can sometimes be grounds for the reduction or elimination of alimony (spousal support) payments.

## B. CHILD CUSTODY

If you and your spouse agree on child custody, the court will normally ratify your agreement (to award custody according to your joint desire) without looking at the details of your life. Remember, the judge won't know whether one of you is living with a third person unless it is brought to his or her attention. However, if you and your spouse are seriously fighting over the question of who shall have custody of your children, the best conservative legal advice has been not to live with a person of the opposite sex and to be very discreet in all your sexual activity, at least until the court has made a decision regarding custody. This advice has applied to both "fault" and "no fault" divorce states as the living arrangements of both parties are always admissible in custody disputes under the theory that a court needs as much information as possible to determine "the best interests of the child".

Perhaps you noted that we used the word "has" in the last paragraph to describe the kind of "no sex no living with anyone" conduct that should be followed by parents engaged in a custody fight. We did this because there has been a considerable relaxation of uptight legal attitudes toward living together in the past few years. While we can't say that most judges are enthusiastic about granting custody to a parent who is living with someone, there is a definite trend away from denying custody for this reason and we feel that a decision as to whether it is wise to live with someone while fighting over child custody must be decided on a situation-by-situation, state-by-state basis.

In all states child custody is decided according to "the best interests of the child." What does this mean? It seems to mean that the judge who hears a disputed custody fight can take into account all the evidence and allegations before him, then decide which party can provide the "best home" for the child. In practice our historical societal prejudice in favor of a mother raising children commonly prevails. However, the almost automatic preference for the mother is not nearly as strong as it once was, and many men are winning custody of their children. Most states now provide that both parents have an equal right to custody with the award made on a "best interests of the child" approach.* In any state, under any test, the trial judge has almost complete discretion in awarding custody where two parents are fighting over the issue.

People frequently ask:

"If I live with a man, can my children be taken from me?"

"If my husband is an alcoholic, will he be able to have the children?"

"I have an arrest for possession of marijuana; does this mean I cannot get the children?"

"My husband does not pay his child support; can he take the children from me?"

"My son is nine years old and wants to live with me; will the court do what he wants?"

"I only earn $10,000 a year and my spouse earns $40,000; does this mean he will get the children?"

"Is it actually possible for a father to get custody of young children?"

---

* In many states "joint custody" is possible. In some it is becoming the preferred way to award custody. We recommend this when parents have a record of good communication and an equal dedication to raising the children. "Joint custody" is advantageous because it equalizes the balance of power among the parents and gives each an equal say in raising the children. In our experience fathers are much more likely to support and maintain close relationships with their children when they are truly involved in decision-making. "Joint custody" means that the parents (and hopefully the children) continue to plan jointly for their children's future just as they did before divorce. Actual physical custody of the children is worked out between the parents, taking into consideration schools, neighborhoods, the children's wishes, etc. "Joint custody" does not mean that the children must spend six months of each year with each parent. A common criticism of joint custody is that since neither parent has the final say, arguments can go on forever even though both parents feel that they are highly motivated to be good parents. This point has some validity and we feel that "joint custody" often works best where parents and children commit themselves to a program of family counseling (sometimes called "divorce" or "separation" counseling) to help them over the rough spots. We haven't seen a whole lot of marriages "saved" by counseling, but have seen many families saved much anguish by separation counseling. Remember, a good divorce can be as precious as a good marriage.

The answer to all these questions is, "It depends." In spite of what your next-door neighbor, your best friend, or your brother-in-law has told you, the law does not say that adultery, smoking pot, drinking, etc. will necessarily result in the loss of custody (in fact, it often does not). It is up to each individual judge to determine who shall get custody, and he or she will necessarily apply his or her own standards (prejudices). Some judges do not like dope; some do not like arrest records; some do not like political activity; some do not like poor people; and some, in spite of prevailing attitudes, do not like unmarried persons living together, although as we noted above, this isn't nearly the no-no it used to be. Each judge is an individual, each case is unique, and the judge has a lot of latitude in deciding each case. People worried about custody sometimes ask if it is better to have their friend live with them and help raise the children, or to have the friend live elsewhere and visit. If you are not fighting over custody, neither is a problem. If you are fighting over custody, neither will do you any good, but we feel that in many communities, in many fact situations, neither dating nor living with someone in a stable relationship will be cause to deny custody. However, there are definitely some states where it will be considered as a negative factor in deciding a contested custody case and a few where it may be used as a reason to deny custody.

In reaching the conclusion that cohabitation is not usually viewed as a reason to deny custody, we have carefully researched the recent case law. While we don't have the space to do a state-by-state breakdown, here are some typical holdings: "We have long passed the point where sexual misconduct automatically disqualifies a mother from obtaining custody of her minor children." *Greenfield v. Greenfield*, 260 N.W.2d 493 (Nebraska 1977). "The fact of the mother's adulterous relationship is of importance in a child custody case only as it may affect the best interests of the child." *Bonjour v. Bonjour* 566 P.2d 667 (Alaska 1977). If you want to research other recent cases in this area, see the Family Law Reporter which you will find in all law libraries. As mentioned, it is still possible however, to find cases from conservative states where a court held cohabitation to be a reason to deny custody, but they are few and getting fewer.*

## 1. Deciding The Contested Custody Case

In most states judges do not decide custody cases simply by inviting the parents to present their rival arguments. Long before the parents even get to court, other governmental agencies are involved. In many states the agency with primary responsibility is the County Juvenile Probation Department. Other states use names such as "Social Services Department" or "Department of Child Welfare", but the functions carried out are similar everywhere.

What normally happens is something like this. The lawyers (or the parties themselves if they are in pro per) notify the court that, as part of a divorce proceeding, there is a fight over custody. The judge then asks the relevant county department to make an

---

* Missouri in *In Re Marriage of J-H-M*, 544 S.W. 582 (1976) and Virginia in *Brown v. Brown*, 237 S.E. 2d 89 (1980) are two states that still find that cohabitation is a reason to deny custody. Illinois has ruled that custody should be denied when a parent with custody lives with someone. De Franco v. De Franco 384, N.E. 2d 997, Jarrett v. Jarrett 400 N.E. 2d 421 (1979). Iowa in *In Re Marriage of Kramer*, 397 N.W. 2d 359 (1980) makes a mother's cohabitation one factor to consider in custody cases.

investigation. The case is assigned to a case worker (almost always trained as a social worker) who investigates the entire situation and presents a written report and recommendation to the court. In the process of investigating, the social worker interviews the parties, assembles background information, collects arrest and health records, checks with references provided by the parties, sometimes talks with the children and sometimes requests psychological testing or psychiatric reports.

Individual social workers have different degrees of skill in interviewing and assessing personalities, and some are more energetic than others. Like judges, social workers have their own biases and a recommendation will reflect the prejudice of the worker as well as what may be considered the "facts" of the situation. While as a whole these investigative personnel are younger and more tolerant than most judges, a social worker will probably feel compelled to mention your living situation in the report. Even though the particular person who did the investigation might not think it important that you are living with a person of the opposite sex, the judge may feel differently.

What happens once a judge receives a child custody report? Your attorney (or you if you represent yourself) will have the opportunity to read the report before court proceedings and discuss it with you. The judge is not compelled to go along with the report, but he or she usually does. If the investigative officer has recommended that you have custody, you have won more than half the battle. If the report recommends that you not have custody of your children, you are at a serious disadvantage, but you are still entitled to a trial on the issue, and you may request that the social worker come to court so that he can be corss-examined about the contents of the report. If, after the report is received, you and your spouse still cannot agree as to who shall have custody of the children, the next step is to have such a trial. At the trial your children may be asked where they want to live. Judges vary on this procedure, with some always asking the children if they feel that they are old enough to answer, and others never talking with the children. As a very general guide, most judges will pay little attention to the opinions of a child under 7, will probably respect the wishes of teen-age children if the chosen parent is otherwise suitable, and will listen to children between 7 and 12, but not necessarily give them what they ask for. There is also a strong tendency for judges to keep brothers and sisters together, although this is not always done.

**CAUTION:** In a custody proceeding held in the context of a divorce or dissolution of marriage, a judge need not award custody of the children to either the husband or the wife; he can award custody to a relative, a friend or even the local juvenile court. This law is noted here to warn hostile parents that too much mud-slinging may, and frequently does, convince the judge that neither parent is fit.

## C. VISITATION OF CHILDREN

Let's say it is agreed that your spouse is to have custody of the children. Unless your physical presence can be shown to be actually detrimental to the welfare of the children, you will be given the right to visit.* If you and your spouse are still friendly

---

* Section 4601 of the California Civil Code is a typical state statute. It reads: *"Reasonable visitation rights shall be awarded to a parent unless it is shown that such visitation would be detrimental to the best interests of the child. In the discretion of the court, reasonable visitation rights may be granted to any other person having an interest in the welfare of the child."*

enough to agree on how the visitation rights are to be exercised, the court will probably say that you have "reasonable visitation rights", and leave it to you to work out times and places. If, however, you and your spouse are at such a bad place that you cannot agree on such simple things as when, where and how the visitation will take place, the court will define visitation rights more or less rigidly. For example, the court may say, "Barbara Washington shall have the right to visit with the children every Saturday from 10:00 a.m. to 5:00 p.m. plus one week during·the summer months, said week to be agreed upon by the parties"; or "Sean Washington shall have the right to visit with the children on the first weekend of every month from 6:00 p.m. on Friday to 6:00 p.m. on Sunday provided that he pick up and deliver the children to the home of Barbara Washington", etc.

Occasionally, a court will impose further restrictions on visitation such as a requirement that the visiting parent tell the other parent of his or her intention to visit 24 hours before the time of visitation, a requirement that the visiting parent not remove the child from the county or the state or, in rare cases, the child's own home or the house of a third party, or a requirement that the visiting parent not drink alcoholic beverages while he is visiting with the children. But, can the court impose a restraint on Sean Washington that he not visit with his children in the presence of Doris Williams (the woman with whom he is living)? Or that his children may not spend the night with him if Ms. Williams is also present in the house? There is little in the way of case law from appeals courts that declare this legal or not; likewise, there are no statutes in this area.* However, even today, some judges occasionally make such orders, supposedly to "protect the children". If you are faced with such an order, you should speak with your attorney as to your obligations and rights and the possibility of appeal. It is rarely wise to violate a court order.

## D. CHILD SUPPORT

What happens if you have custody of the children and you are living with someone else? Is your spouse or former spouse still required to support the children? YES, but read on.**

In theory, child support depends on two factors:

**1. The ability to pay of the parent who does not have custody.** You cannot get out of child support by quitting your job or refusing to look for work. Court orders are made and enforced on the basis of ability to work, not inclination to work.

Here is a rough guide used by judges in Marin County, California in deciding how much child support to order in an individual case. Judges rarely follow this schedule exactly, or the similar ones in use in other counties, since the facts (human needs and responsibilities) of each situation vary. Please note that these figures don't include spousal support. This is because spousal support is awarded much less frequently

---

* In Florida, the Court of Appeals has declared that the mere fact of a father's cohabitation should not terminate his overnight visitation with his five-year-old child unless there is a showing that the living together situation has an adverse impact upon the child's welfare. *Hackley v. Hackley*, 6 FLR 2022.

** Failure to support your children if you have the ability to do so is a crime in all states. Many people who don't take their obligation seriously end up with a free education at a county school with high grey walls and bars on the windows.

than it used to be, as most younger women are wage earners.

## SCHEDULE FOR CHILD SUPPORT PAYMENTS WHERE NO SPOUSAL SUPPORT IS ORDERED

| Non-custodial Parent's NET Monthly Income* | One Child | Two Children | Three or More Children |
|---|---|---|---|
| $ 400.00 | $ 100.00 | $ 100.00 | $ 100.00 |
| 500.00 | 125.00 | 150.00 | 175.00 |
| 600.00 | 150.00 | 200.00 | 225.00 |
| 700.00 | 150.00 | 250.00 | 275.00 |
| 800.00 | 150.00 | 250.00 | 300.00 |
| 900.00 | 175.00 | 275.00 | 350.00 |
| 1000.00 | 175.00 | 300.00 | 375.00 |
| 1200.00 | 200.00 | 350.00 | 450.00 |
| 1400.00 | 250.00 | 400.00 | 525.00 |
| 1600.00 | 250.00 | 450.00 | 600.00 |
| 1800.00 | 275.00 | 500.00 | 675.00 |
| 2000.00 | 300.00 | 550.00 | 750.00 |
| Above 2000.00 | Court's discretion | | |

This schedule is prepared on the assumption that the custodial parent's net earnings are at least 25% less than that of the non-custodial parent, and that there is no award of spousal support.

The rule for support is intended to be the same whether the custodial parent is the father or the mother. If the non-custodial parent carries hospital, medical or dental insurance covering the children, the cost attributable to the children's coverage may be deducted from the support payments.

**2. The needs of the children.** The person with whom you are living has no obligation to support your children. Logically, the amount of child support the father (or mother, if the father has custody) is ordered to pay should not be affected by the fact that you are living with someone else. However, if such person is actually providing shelter or buying food or clothing or other items for your children, this might possibly be taken into consideration by the court when it decides how much money the non-custodial parent will have to pay.

**EXAMPLE:** Barbara Washington and Sean Washington get a divorce and the custody of the two children is awarded to Barbara with reasonable rights of visitation awarded to Sean. Sean is ordered to pay Barbara $200 per month per child for child support. A year later Barbara starts living with (or marries, it makes no difference)

---

* Income after compulsory deductions such as income tax, FICA, SDI and compulsory retirement.

Harold, who owns his own business and nets $100,000 per year. Harold takes an interest in the children and spends money on them freely. Barbara continues working at her job as a librarian. Sean petitions the court and asks that the amount of his support obligation be reduced to $125 per month. Will he succeed? Perhaps, because Barbara is now living in a situation where there is more than adequate money. While the judge will not require Harold to support Sean's children and is not supposed to look at the money that he actually contributes (in fact he or she probably will), the court is required to look at Barbara's total financial picture. As Harold and all of his money are part of Barbara's life, a judge might well rule that Barbara could now spend more of her own income to support the children.*

---

* One California court has ruled that if a married couple signs an agreement to keep all earnings and other property separate, a court can't consider their joint income in evaluating the ability of one of them to support children from a prior relationship, but must only examine the ability to support of that parent.

What if you are the parent without custody and you are living with someone? How does this affect the amount of child support you will be ordered to pay? Perhaps you are actually supporting the person with whom you are living and maybe even that person's children, in whole or in part. Legally, you have no obligation to support these persons and few judges will allow the fact of such support to in any way reduce the support you will be ordered to pay for your natural children. The law clearly states that your primary duty is to support your own children and not someone else or their children. Likewise, if your own living expenses are reduced by the fact that you share rent, etc. with another person, this will be taken into account in determining your ability to pay.

**NOTE:** We have seen this area of the law work great hardship on people who were honestly trying to be decent and caring. For example, this situation often occurs when a man gets a divorce and lives with another woman and her children whom he helps to support in the absence of their father who has skipped. This, of course, does not free him of his legal duty to support his original family even if his former wife has remarried. He will be hauled into court if he fails to do so. Thus, one man trying to do right finds himself with an impossible burden while others avoid doing even part of their share. We don't have any magic answers to this problem, but we do feel that laws causing so much hardship should be re-examined in the light of what life is really like these days. We are particularly concerned that present laws result in a massive, but uneven and often unfair, shifting of money from one family to another, with a great deal of the money sticking to the fingers of the shifters — lawyers, social workers, court personnel and all sorts of other bureaucrats.

**IMPORTANT:** Most states are tightening requirements regarding child support. For example, California has enacted a law which states that, if an absent parent falls behind two months in his child support payments, the judge **must** make an order assigning his wages. This means that the absent parent's employer will be required to pay the amount of the child support directly to the custodial parent or some official agency. The absent parent will never see this money in his paycheck. Also, cooperation between states in collecting child support from persons who move to another part of the country is becoming more efficient. This involves the use of federal government computers to trace people through social security numbers, etc.

## E. SPOUSAL SUPPORT (ALIMONY)

Alimony, a necessary concept a generation ago when papa went to the office and mama stayed home to tend the babies and the spaghetti, is dying as lifestyles change. Among younger people especially, alimony is no longer routinely granted and is not even requested in a large number of cases. Any alimony (spousal support) that you do receive will terminate upon your remarriage, in the absence of a specific agreement or court order to the contrary. What happens if you do not remarry but just move in with someone else? The rules vary state-to-state. In New York, living with someone is not grounds to end alimony **unless the living together relationship has lasted six months**

**and the woman receiving alimony holds herself out as being the wife of the person she is living with.** However, in California a recent law change (Civil Code 4801.51) states: "Except as otherwise agreed to by the parties in writing, there shall be a rebuttable presumption...of decreased need for support if the supported party is cohabiting with a person of the opposite sex. Upon such a finding of changed circumstances, the court may modify the payment of support..." *

**RESEARCH NOTE:** If receiving alimony is important to you, don't live with someone unless you thoroughly check out the current law in your state. The trend of state law is probably to restrict or eliminate alimony when the person receiving the alimony lives with someone, but many states impose no restrictions. Go to a public law library (in the county courthouse) and get a copy of your state's laws.** These come in many volumes, and you will want to start with the index. Look at the headings under Alimony and Spousal Support. Be sure to check the back of the index to see if there are any staple-bound pages (called pocket parts) which contain recent law changes. Check with the librarian to be sure that you are looking at up-to-date material. Also, ask the law librarian if there are any books on the domestic relations law of your state. All of the big states will have them. For example, in California, they are published by Continuing Education of the BAR (CEB). Also ask the librarian to refer you to the Family Law Reporter which contains a digest of case law decisions. If you are in doubt, check your conclusions with a lawyer (see Chapter 12).

## F. DIVIDING THE PROPERTY

If you were married for more than a few minutes, you and your spouse probably accumulated both property and debts. Property includes houses, other real property such as improved land, furniture, cars, motorcycles, savings accounts, checking accounts, stocks, copyrights, patents, bonds, income tax refunds, money owed you by other persons, interests in retirement funds or pensions, some kinds of disability benefits, vacation pay earned during the marriage, businesses you or your spouse may have operated, etc. Whether the property will be divided by the court depends on when it was acquired, whether your state recognizes community property, the interests of other persons in the property, etc. In "community property" states most property and debts acquired after marriage are divided equally between the husband and the wife. In other states "equitable distribution" laws often achieve the same result. In many of these, however, the fact a judge has discretion in deciding who gets what (and in a few states can still consider who is at fault) is more likely to result in a contested trial.

If you live in a state where property division is not automatically 50-50 and you have a large amount of property which you and your spouse cannot agree on how to divide, you should settle yourself in for a long, tedious bettle and start saving money

---

\* As this book goes to press Alabama is the only other state to adopt legislation to provide for termination of alimony when the person receiving it lives with someone. However, the question has also been considered by a number of state courts, some of which have cut-off alimony, some of which have refused to do so and some of which have made different rulings depending on the circumstances.

\*\*People unfamiliar with legal research will want to look at Elias, *How to Find and Understand the Law*, Nolo Press.

for your lawyer's fees. Of course, if you and your spouse have already agreed on a reasonable division of the property in view of the needs and earning capabilities of each person, then you should not allow lawyers or others to talk you into a needless fight. Remember, divorce lawyers, like gunfighters, often get more money and power when they fight than when they show you how to arrive at an early compromise.

If you are already divorced when you start living with another person, it is almost certain that your property from your marriage is already divided. In this case, you do not have to worry about the court changing its decision if someone tells the judge you are living with someone. The decision has been made, and the matter cannot be reopened. However, if you are not yet divorced, and the state you live in does not have a no fault divorce system, and you and your spouse are fighting over the division of the property, then you can be sure your living situation will be brought to the attention of the judge. Your adultery, desertion, abandonment and infliction of mental cruelty will be taken into consideration with the other facts of the case and may influence the court's decision.

## G. AFTER THE DIVORCE

Your marriage is now legally finished; you are settling down to a new life with your new partner. Can you forget about all the above because now the court has made its orders regarding child custody, visitation, child support, and spousal support? NO. All orders regarding the above matters except those pertaining to the division of the property may be changed by the court if it finds that the circumstances have changed since the making of the original order.

EXAMPLE: At the time you were awarded custody of the children, you were a Sunday School teacher whose only recreation was to attend Sunday afternoon piccolo concerts. Now you and your children are living in a commune for ex-alcoholic slide trombone players. Can your former spouse ask the court to change custody and does the court have the power to do so? Yes. Will the court change custody? Perhaps, depending on what the judge thinks of your current lifestyle. You will have less trouble if you can show that the children are secure, well taken care of, and doing OK in school; but you have a serious problem if it looks as though you are trying to raise kids in an unstructured zoo.

EXAMPLE: At the time of the dissolution you were a medical student with no income but now you are a doctor earning $90,000 per year. Can your ex-spouse ask the court to raise the amount of child support and/or alimony and does the court have the power to do so? Yes. Will it do so? Almost certainly.

EXAMPLE: At the time of the divorce you earned $25,000 per year as a bricklayer and you lost your job a couple of months ago. Can you ask the court to lower the amount of child support you were ordered to pay? Yes. Will the court grant what you want? Perhaps, depending on why you lost your job, your chances of getting another job, your current sources of income, etc.

What can you do to keep your former spouse from taking you back to court? Very little. Your ex-spouse has the right to petition the court to change its order on child custody, support and visitation at any time. You have the same right. Your best course of action is to maintain amicable relations with your ex-spouse. For example, if you are extremely cooperative about visitation, your ex-spouse will probably be less likely to petition the court to change custody if your lifestyle changes. Likewise, if you are prompt and reasonably generous with your child support and alimony payments, your ex-spouse is much less likely to hassle you about visitation. If your income goes up (or down) you and your former spouse should try to work out a voluntary change of the support amount. If you do, you should make a note of it.

---

### SAMPLE SUPPORT CHANGE AGREEMENT*

Sean Washington of 100 South Street, El Monte, California, and Barbara Washington of 57 San Pablo Avenue, Redding, California, make the following agreement regarding the support of their two minor children, John Washington and Richard Washington:

1. That because Sean Washington has suffered a serious illness which has reduced his income by 50%, it is agreed that the $800 per month child support ordered in the divorce action between the parties is too high.

2. In order to avoid an expensive court proceeding to lower child support, and because Sean Washington's health problems should improve in the next six months, it is agreed that Sean Washington will pay to Barbara Washington the sum of $325 per month for the support of John and Richard commencing May 1, 19    and terminating with the payment of November 1, 19    and that all additional amounts of support for this time are forever given up by Barbara Washington.

3. It is further agreed that the full amount of support ordered as part of the divorce proceedings ($800) will be paid commencing December 1, 19

| | |
|---|---|
| Date | Sean Washington |
| Date | Barbara Washington |

---

* It is not necessary to notarize this sort of agreement, but it would be a good idea to do so. If one or the other person fails to live up to it, it may be necessary to present it in court in which case it may carry more weight if notarized. If you believe that your former spouse may not live up to the agreement, you should have a court ratify the change from the beginning. In California you can easily do this yourself following the instructions in Matthews, *After the Divorce*, Nolo Press. In other states you will have to check procedures at the law library. See Chapter 12.

## SAMPLE SUPPORT CHANGE AGREEMENT

Hermione Brown of 6 Briar Close, Larchmont, New York and Cecil Brown of 11 Brookside Drive, Mamaroneck, New York agree as follows:

1. That because Cecil Brown has received a promotion and is now receiving $4,000 per year more than was received at the time of the original court child support order entered on_____ ;

and

2. That in order to avoid the expense of a court appearance to modify child support to an amount that is fair, taking into consideration Cecil's increase in income;

3. The parties hereby agree that Cecil shall pay Hermione the amount of $375 per month for the support of each child commencing May 1, 19    and continuing indefinitely or until the parties jointly agree on a modification.

| | |
|---|---|
| _____ | _____ |
| Date | Cecil Brown |
| _____ | _____ |
| Date | Hermione Brown |

**NOTE:** If you and your former spouse are planning to agree on a permanent change in support and you have had problems with misunderstandings in the past, you will probably wish to take your agreement to a lawyer and have him or her present it to the court in the form of a "stipulated" or agreed upon modification. As long as you are in agreement, this shouldn't take the attorney more than three or four hours total and shouldn't cost a great deal.

Every year many attorneys get rich because two people cannot sit down and work out their domestic problems. When problems first arise, try to talk them out with your ex-spouse, maybe giving a little more than you had planned. Try not to let your pride or ego get in the way of making an agreement. Only if this fails should you contact an attorney and pay him many hundreds (often thousands) of dollars to fight for you. In our experience attorneys don't normally arrive at better solutions — just solutions that take longer and cost more.

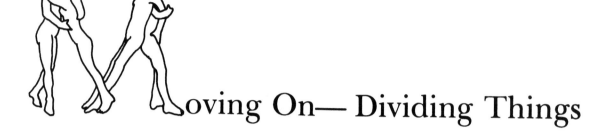

# oving On— Dividing Things

## A. ON BEING HUMAN

Even the nicest relationships come to an end. Whether you leave one another with good or bad feelings is probably largely dependent on how you feel about yourselves at the time. Still, no matter how sensitive, caring and giving each of you is, there are likely to be some sticky moments. The loss of an important part of your life can't help but affect you in powerful ways. It is easy to allow this feeling of loss (anger, hostility, guilt, resentment) to manifest itself in bitter arguments over who will get the coffee pot, dessert forks, children or house. Take a moment now if you are in this situation and think of how you would advise your closest friends, should they be breaking up. Now, see if you are applying this advice to yourself.

It used to be that many people were pressured by door-to-door salesmen into signing expensive contracts for things that they didn't really want. A signature on a contract at a moment of emotional overeagerness, and the unlucky buyer found himself faced with many months (or years) of payments. Eventually, Congress dealt with this kind of injustice with a law that provided a person signing one of these contracts a three-day "cooling-off period" during which he could cancel the contract without the necessity of giving a reason. The idea was that folks should not be stuck permanently with their own hasty actions committed in an emotion-charged atmosphere. We think this is a good plan to follow in breaking off a relationship. You have had an argument, you are both tired of each other, and you have both very likely said things to hurt the other. Don't stomp out with your back scratcher and the check books and announce you will never return. Give yourself three days (at least) to "cool off", either in the apartment or house or somewhere else. If, after this time, you are still convinced that you want to split and you are both able to discuss matters rationally, sit down and

divide. But, if one of you still cannot talk without fighting or crying, wait another week or so before you again try to settle the financial matters. Of course, division of property, etc. is not important compared to what is really going on, but, a year from now, **you** will feel better if you think you got your fair share of the material items. Also, more importantly, you will not be able to complain bitterly about your financial losses and fool yourself that this is what really concerns you.

One of the authors was once contacted by a man in his forties who was being sued for divorce by his wife of twenty years. The wife had asked for custody of the minor children and, from the information volunteered by the husband, it seemed likely that the court would follow her wishes. There were many bills, but few assets other than the furniture and an automobile. The man bitterly complained, "What have I got to show for 20 years of marriage?" The author suggested that he had lived twenty years in a close relationship. Some of these years were good, and many of them were enjoyable, and he had children who continued to love him even though they preferred living with their mother. Living together, whether married or not, is not an investment, it is a shared experience. The question is not what you have at the end of the relationship, but what happiness you enjoyed and were able to give while it lasted. If you were together for some time, you did it because that was what you wanted.

Every attorney who does any domestic work is all too familiar with the client who files for a divorce announcing he or she wants everything he or she can get, refuses to accept any reasonable offer of settlement, obtains a judgment and continues to be dissatisfied, no matter how favorable the court's decision was. This kind of person travels from lawyer to lawyer, seeking to have the case re-opened, castigating the spouse, the previous attorneys, and the judge for their share in the "humiliation". This sort of person never lets go, continues to make himself (or herself) knowledgeable as to the whereabouts and actions of the other spouse and never lets an opportunity for a little gratuitous harrassment pass. Commonly this type of bitterness leads to fights over support until the children have become adults and the spouse remarries or dies. Payments are not made on time or in full, and the spouse is continually going to court to attempt to change the support order.

The sight is not pretty. It takes only a minimal knowledge of psychology for the outsider to evaluate what is really happening. Don't let yourself get involved in this sort of bitter craziness. It is so easy to become a prisoner of your own bad feelings and not always so easy to stay in touch with your humanity. **It is not worth** engaging in marathon battles particularly if the other person is as bad as you say he (she) is.


## B. PROPERTY

If you have paid attention to Chapters 3, 5 and 7 of this book and have been careful to order your economic affairs along the lines of any one of the sample property agreements we have given you, you're in good shape — maybe not emotionally, but at least materially. Dividing things up according to the guidelines you yourselves have set up should not be difficult. If you do run into problems due to a conflicting interpretation of one or more contract clauses, consider getting a neutral third person to help you make a compromise. Going to court to fight over property almost always costs more than the property is worth, so you have every incentive to compromise even if you end up with less than you believe to be reasonable.

But what happens if you and your partner never wrote down anything **and** you have accumulated assets and debts? If, after discussing property division with your friend and making every effort to divide things fairly you are unable to reach complete agreement, you should do one of the following:

1. Consider simply forgetting about the whole thing and letting your friend take what he (she) wants. We strongly advise this course if the disputed items are not valuable. We have seen thousands of cases where the objects of dispute were not worth a fight. Also, a little generosity often works wonders in getting your friend to be more reasonable.

2. Consult a third party, together if possible (an attorney may be helpful if you are unclear as to the law), with the idea of working out a compromise.

3. Engage in an all-out war, each with an attorney, involving court fights, etc. We recommend this last course of action if there is a great deal at stake **or** if you feel sorry for lawyers and want to give them all your money. However, if you decide to go this route, you will want to know what law exists governing the property rights and obligations of unmarried couples. Here is where the *Marvin v. Marvin* case comes in again. Re-read Chapter 4 carefully and decide if your situation resembles any of those that would qualify you to claim an implied agreement or partnership or any of the other equitable remedies that are discussed. If you feel you have a worthwhile case, see an attorney. As you must understand by now, this is a highly complex, changing area of the law. Most lawyers know little about it, so if you do wish to go to court you will have to investigate carefully to find someone knowledgeable. But remember, lawsuits take a lot of time and cost a lot of money. The wheels of justice do not spin quickly — indeed, they barely move. Fundamental court reform giving people reasonable access to their own dispute resolution process is way overdue.

## C. PATERNITY

Before reaching the question of custody some people will first have to cope with a father who refuses to acknowledge that he is the father. Yes, this is a nasty situation as well as being a serious legal problem if you do not have an acknowledgment of paternity such as the one in Chapter 8. If you are faced with this problem, or if you will need financial support to raise the children properly and the other parent refuses to pay such support, you should see an attorney, or if you have little money, the district attorney. Paternity actions are unpleasant, but children should not have to suffer because their father is irresponsible.

## D. SUPPORT FOR DEPENDENTS

If you and your partner have had children together, and if you are to have custody, you will want to be sure that you have enough money to support them. Many parents regularly contribute to the support of their children even if they do not have custody, without the necessity of a court order. You are fortunate people if you have the good sense to work out a voluntary support, visitation and custody agreement (see Chapter 8). However, please remember that a "promise" cannot be enforced legally if the

paying parent decides differently in the future. If you believe that there is any possibility that support will not be provided voluntarily, you will need a court order.

Hopefully, when the child was born, the father signed an acknowledgment of paternity statement as described in Chapter 8. If he did not do so, it is extremely important that he do this before you two say good-bye. Even if your break-up is bitter, you must take care to protect the rights of your children. Assuming the father has signed the statement, and that while you were living together the question of support never arose, you are now going to have to deal with some hard facts of life. First try to work out an appropriate amount for the child support contribution. To do this both parents should sit down together. The parent who will have custody of the children should list her (his) monthly income and monthly expenses of the children. Be realistic. Your children need adequate food, clothing, shelter, education including entertainment, and a feeling of security. You are not out to get the other parent and you are not out to be a martyr; you are trying to deal seriously with the future of your children. The parent who will not have custody should also list his monthly income from all sources and his monthly expenses. It may be that your estimates are fairly close and the parent without custody will agree to pay the difference between the income and the expenses of the parent with custody. Re-read Chapters 8 and 9 which contain considerable information on children, support, visitation, etc. If you are not able to arrive at a mutually agreeable solution, the parent with custody may be forced to hire an attorney to get adequate support. This is silly since your children need the money more than the lawyer does. Try again to work out a settlement. There are three alternative custody and support agreements included in Section E of Chapter 8. Read them through thoroughly before writing out your own agreement.

**REMEMBER:** Most low and middle income families cannot realistically expect to support two households on one income. This means that if there is only one wage earner, no one is going to have enough money to be comfortable. We have seen thousands of cases where, with all the good faith in the world, there simply is not enough money to go around. What can we say to help? Not much, except to urge you to pay attention to your friend's needs as well as your own, to try to avoid being paranoid or vindictive, and to remember that in addition to a decent place to live, good food and a feeling of being loved, there is something in the soul of a child that needs a lollipop once in a while.

## E. SUPPORT FOR ONE ANOTHER

It is not uncommon that when people separate there is a mutual understanding that in fairness one owes the other some support. This commonly occurs when one person has been paying the other's school expenses and the breakup happens before the money is repaid. We discuss making an agreement to cover this possibility in advance in Chapter 5. Often, however, people don't plan ahead and must do the best they can in the here and now.

If you have decided that one person will continue to support the other person for a period of time, you should sign an agreement to this effect. Here are two samples:

---

### SAMPLE SEPARATION AGREEMENT

Roger Bane and Mildred Perkins have decided to live separately from this time on. For the past five years they have lived together and Mildred has provided many household services for Roger and has foregone any paid employment.

It is hereby agreed between the parties that commencing March 1, 19    and continuing for a period of one year Roger shall pay to Mildred the sum of $250 a month for a total of $3,000. Said payments shall be made on the first of every month.

| | |
|---|---|
| _____ | _____ |
| Date | Roger Bane |
| _____ | _____ |
| Date | Mildred Perkins |

---

## SAMPLE SEPARATION AGREEMENT

Sue Jessup and Eric Smallwood agree as follows:

1. That for most of the last three years Eric has supported Sue while she got her Doctor of Divinity degree and that the amount of support provided was approximately $18,000.

2. That commencing July 1, 19___ Sue will pay Eric $450 per month. Payments shall be made on the first of each month and shall continue for a total of forty months.


| | |
|---|---|
| _____ | _____ |
| Date | Sue Jessup |
| _____ | _____ |
| Date | Eric Smallwood |

---

Like other agreements, these should be prepared in duplicate. Notarization is optional unless the contracts involve real property, but it never hurts. This sort of support agreement is in the form of a contract and can be enforced in court. If your friend (perhaps we should say former friend) will not sign this kind of agreement and you believe that in fairness he or she should, there remains the possibility of initiating a court action. Depending on the state you will either have to establish an express (oral or written) contract, or may be able to rely on one or another equitable remedy (see Chapter 4).

**TAX CONSEQUENCES:** If money paid by one member of an unmarried couple to the other upon separation is payment for past services the money is deductible by the person making the payment and taxable to the person receiving it. But if the money was transferred as part of an income sharing agreement, or just because one person needed it, and the other was generous the tax law treats the payment as a gift. This means that the person receiving the money has no tax liability, but the person who makes the payments must pay gift tax if the amount paid exceeds $10,000 per year. Of course there are no tax consequences if a payment can be characterized as a loan repayment, unless interest is involved.

## F. CUSTODY OF CHILDREN

If you can't even get to the question of child support because you and your partner cannot agree who should have custody of the children, re-read Chapters 8 and 9 on child custody and starting a family. If you still can't work out a custody agreement, try to get a third party to help. A family counselor may be of great assistance in working out a sensible compromise, fair to all. Only if all else fails, see an attorney. It is very difficult to represent yourself in a contested custody situation (see Chapter 12).

## CONCLUSION

When you have taken care of the property, debts, custody and support of children, you have come through one of the most important and toughest periods of your life. Probably you have had to call on more maturity, patience, intelligence and plain courage than you thought you had. Congratulations.

eath

## A. INHERITANCE RIGHTS OF UNMARRIED COUPLES

Many of us turn off when the subject of death is raised, no matter what the context. We act as though, by ignoring death's inevitability, we can somehow get death to ignore our mortality. This reaction to death is so prevalent that our society has passed laws to cope with it. They are called "intestate succession" laws and are designed to pass the property (less a healthy chunk for the tax man, of course) of those who themselves make no provision to do so, to their relatives.

**It is particularly important for unmarried couples to understand that, according to the "intestate succession" laws of all fifty states, they (i.e., their relationship) does not exist and that, unless they take sensible steps to protect themselves, are extremely likely to be screwed.** In all states, in the absence of a will, one member of a **married** couple will inherit at least part of the estate of the other spouse if there is no divorce decree. Likewise, the spouse will enjoy considerable protections even if the other spouse attempts to give away all the property to some other person or organization in a will. In no state does a person who has been living with another have a right to any property of that person if he (or she) dies without leaving a will.* Children born to unmarried couples who have been legitimated (a paternity statement does this in most states, but in New York and some other states a court proceeding is necessary) will inherit absent a will or other estate planning devices, but here too it is wise to be on the safe side and specifically provide for the children by use of a will or trust or joint ownership or insurance plan such as those mentioned in this chapter.

**EXAMPLE:** Keija and Felix live together for ten years. Each accumulates $50,000 in their own separate bank accounts. They are saving this money for their joint future, but have made no contracts or wills. A brick falls on Felix's head killing him instantly.

---

* A surviving member of an unmarried couple may be able to claim that an oral contract like those discussed in Chapters 2 and 3 existed by which they claim ownership of some of what otherwise would be the deceased's property. We discuss this possibility in Section G of this chapter.

His only blood relative is Aunt Tillie in Omaha, Nebraska whom he hasn't seen in fifteen years and whom he doesn't like. Who inherits, Keija or Tillie? You guessed it — Tillie.

## B. DEFINITIONS

Now that we have established the idea that unmarried couples must do some planning if they wish to leave property to each other, let's learn the meaning of a few terms. Please pay attention (try putting your head under a cold shower half-way through) as the legal gobbledygook relating to death and dying is both specialized and necessary to an understanding of what we are talking about.

ADMINISTRATION (OF AN ESTATE)—the distribution of the estate of a deceased person. The person who manages the distribution is an ADMINISTRATOR (male) or ADMINISTRATRIX (female).

BENEFICIARY—the person or organization who is entitled to receive benefits. Often used in trusts.

CODOCIL—a supplement to a will containing a modification, amendment, explanation, etc.

COMMUNITY PROPERTY — exists in Arizona, California, Idaho, Nevada, New Mexico, Louisiana, Texas and Washington only; consists of that property which is acquired by either party during marriage unless the property is inherited or given to one's spouse as a gift.

ESTATE—all the property of a person who has died.

HEIR—a person who inherits.

HOLOGRAPHIC WILL—a will that is completely handwritten. Such a will is valid in many states. (See Section D, below.)

INHERIT—to receive from someone who has died.

ISSUE—the children and descendants of a person.

INTESTATE—without a will. To die intestate means to die without having a will. INTESTATE SUCCESSION is the way property of a deceased person is distributed if the deceased did not leave a valid will.

LIFE ESTATE—the right to use property, most often real property, during one's lifetime. This is a valuable property interest short of absolute ownership.

PERSONAL PROPERTY—all property which is not real property.

PER CAPITA—a method of dividing an estate between relatives in use in many states. You will see it used in this chapter in the chart outlining the laws of the various states if you die without a will. For example: if a de-

159

ceased person died intestate leaving five grandchildren, three of whom were the children of a deceased child and two of whom were the children of another deceased child and the grandparent died in a "per capita" state, each grandchild would receive one-fifth of the estate. **Per capita is another way to say "in equal shares."**

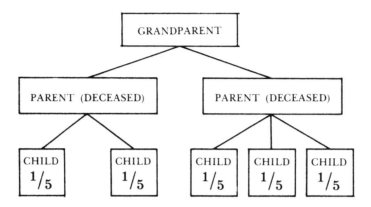

PER STIRPES—(By right of representation) a method of dividing an estate between relatives in use in many states. It is somewhat different from the "per capita" system. As with "per capita" above, it is important in this chapter in understanding the laws of the various states if you die without a will. For example: if a deceased person died intestate leaving five grandchildren, three of whom were the children of a deceased child, and two of whom were the children of another deceased child, and the grandparent died in a "per stirpes" state, the three children of the one deceased child would divide one-half of the estate and the two children of the other deceased child would divide the other one-half.

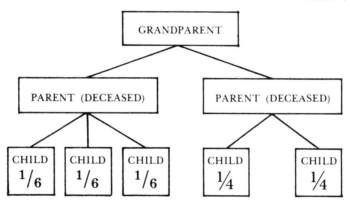

PROBATE—the name for the court procedure designed to prove a will authentic and distribute the property according to the will.

REAL PROPERTY—land and those items attached to the land such as buildings, etc.

RESIDUE—that which is left when something is taken out.

160

SEPARATE PROPERTY—in states which have community property laws, that property which is not community property.

SIBLINGS—brothers and sisters.

SUCCESSION—who gets what when someone dies. THE LAWS OF SUCCESSION are the laws which regulate who will share in the estate.

SURVIVE—to be living when someone dies.

TESTATE—to die testate is to die with a valid will.

TESTATOR—person leaving property by will.

TRUST—a relationship in which one person (the trustee) holds title (often subject to a number of conditions) to property for the benefit of another person (the beneficiary). A trust is commonly used when money is left to people inexperienced in its management such as children or as a tax saving device.

WILL—a legal document in which a person states who he wants to inherit his property.

## C. INTESTATE SUCCESSION: WHAT HAPPENS TO YOUR PROPERTY IF YOU DIE WITHOUT A WILL?

### 1. Introduction

Before discussing the various ways that you can leave your property, let's first understand what happens if you don't leave a will or adopt some other device to pass property such as "joint tenancy." What happens depends a good deal on the state you and your property are located in. All states have systems of "intestate succession" that will pass your property to your relatives if you have any, and to the state if you don't. Most are very similar. If you want to know what your state law provides, go to a public library or law library and get a copy of your state's legal code. Look under the index heading for "intestate succession." If this doesn't work try "Descent and Distribution." If you find that the intestate succession law of your state works to leave your property to exactly who you want to receive it, there is no pressing need to prepare a will. But remember, both leaving property under a will or by intestate succession ends up requiring that your property go through probate in most states. Many people wish to avoid the time and expense of probate and thus pass their property in other ways. See Section E of this chapter.

**IMPORTANT:** Before you can make an intelligent will or some other arrangement to pass on your property at death, you have to know what property is yours. Don't laugh. This can sometimes be a tough one. If you have lived with a person for a long time, your property may have gotten so mixed up with your friend's that it is difficult to tell who owns what. If you find yourselves in this situation and have a reasonably small amount of property, it would be a good idea to sit down with your friend and make an agreement as to who owns what. Have the agreement notarized. If large amounts of property are involved, you may want to get professional help.

## SAMPLE PROPERTY OWNERSHIP AGREEMENT

Felix Finnegan and Keija Adams agree as follows:

1. That they have been living together for ten years and that during that time much of their real and personal property has become mixed together so that it is not completely clear who owns what;*

2. That the purpose of this agreement is to divide all of Keija's and Felix's real and personal property into two categories as set out below;**

3. That it is agreed that, from the date this agreement is signed by both parties, all property listed in category 1 belongs solely and absolutely to Felix and that all property listed in category 2 belongs solely and absolutely to Keija;

Category 1 (Felix)

1. 198_ Ford
2. G.E. Washer & Dryer
3. 100 Shares of stock in Melt-
   in-Your-Mouth Popcorn, Inc.
4. Etc.
5. Etc.

Category 2 (Keija)

1. 198_ Yamaha Cycle
2. BMX Stereo & related stereo equipment
3. $12,000 in the Restaurant Worker
   Credit Union
4. Etc.
5. Etc.

_____          _____
Date                              Keija Adams

_____          _____
Date                              Felix Finnegan

                    Notarize

---

* Where real property is involved, you will want to be sure that ownership of the property on the title slip conforms with this agreement.
** It would also be possible to set up a third category for property owned jointly. If you do this, each piece of property and how it is owned should be listed. For example, "House at 1547 Jones St. in joint tenancy".

162

## 2. Details of Intestate Succession

We do not give you a list of the intestate succession laws of every state both because of space considerations and because we believe you should either complete a will or use one or another of the estate planning devices to pass your property discussed in this chapter.

However, this is what would happen to your property in many states assuming you are single.*

• If you have a child (or children) all your property would go to your child (or children) and would be divided equally if you have more than one. The only exception to this rule would be if one or more of your children died before you do leaving grandchildren. These grandchildren would take per stirpes (or by right of representation). This concept is explained in the Definitions Section of this chapter.

• If you leave no children or grandchildren when you die the property goes all to your parent or equally to your parents if they are alive.

• Next in line are your brothers and sisters who share equally unless one or more is dead leaving issue in which case the issue (your nieces and nephews) of the deceased sister or brother share with your living sisters and brothers per stirpes (by right of representation). See Definitions Section of this chapter.

• If you leave no kids, grandchildren, parents or brothers or sisters, your nephews and nieces share your estate equally unless you have grandnephews and grandnieces of a dead niece or nephew in which case they take by right of representation.

• If you have none of the above relatives your estate passes half to your paternal grandparents and half to your maternal grandparents. If they are dead their issue take equally (these are your parents first cousins and your first cousins once removed). Should any of these first cousins be dead the property goes to their issue by right of representation (these are your second cousins).

• If you have none of these relatives the property goes to the state.

**WARNING:** Don't rely on the above for more than general information. Details vary state to state. Look up yours in your state probate code if you want your local details. Remember, if you make your own will or alternative estate plan you may leave your property to anyone you wish to including the person you are living with.

---

* Remember, you are not single unless you have a final decree of divorce. If you die intestate still married to someone they will inherit a large part of your property.

## D. MAKING A WILL

If you are not happy with the intestate succession scheme in your state (and most unmarried couples will not be) you will want to consider alternative ways to dispose of your property. One common method is by making a will. Wills work well to pass small amounts of property, but like intestate succession, wills result in property going through probate. In Section E below, we will briefly discuss some ways to leave property that avoid probate.

There are commonly two kinds of wills: "witnessed wills" and "holographic wills". A witnessed will is usually prepared by an attorney who knows the proper procedures and forms. Most states are quite fussy about the number of witnesses who must be present and the language that must be used. If you have a large estate, you need to do some homework especially on the tax consequences of your acts.* Once you know what the rules are, you may wish to have a lawyer help you with the paperwork.

A holographic will is one that is dated, written and signed entirely in your own handwriting. It must not be typewritten nor may any typewriting appear on the will. No other writing or printing other than your own may appear on the will.** Holographic wills are valid only in the following states: Alaska, Arizona, Arkansas, California, Colorado, Florida, Hawaii, Idaho, Kentucky, Louisiana, Maine, Michigan, Minnesota, Mississippi, Montana, Nebraska, Nevada, New Mexico, North Carolina, North Dakota, Oklahoma, Pennsylvania, South Dakota, Tennesse, Texas, Utah, Virginia, West Virginia and Wyoming. In these states a holographic will is just as valid as the kind the attorney prepares. You do not have to use any formal language and only need to be careful that you write what you intend.*** However in some states a holographic will is not valid unless it is dated. An example of a holographic will follows.

**WARNING:** Let us repeat: Holographic wills are fine for small estates; however for large ones, especially where someone may contest the will, there can be problems proving that the signature on the will is really that of the deceased. For these and other reasons, it is not wise to use a holographic will if you are leaving a big estate.

**IMPORTANT:** You may change your will at any time. The simplest way of doing this is to physically destroy the original will and all copies when you make your new will. If this can't be done, you may revoke a former will by specifically stating that you are doing so in a later will. Your will should be kept in a safe deposit box or other safe place. Be careful that no one who benefits from the will has physical possession of it as this can create nasty legal problems. It is fine to give a beneficiary a summary of the will so that he or she may know where he or she stands at your death.

---

* We don't have the space here to deal with estate taxes and ways to avoid them. Basically, you are exempt from federal estate tax liability after 1984 if your total estate is less than $400,000. We recommend *Federal Estate and Gift Taxes Explained*, New York, Commerce Clearing House, for a detailed discussion of federal tax law. For state tax information, contact your state tax collector. Californians and Texans have an even better source of information, Clifford, *Plan Your Estate: Wills, Probate Avoidance, Trusts & Taxes* (Texas and California Editions), Nolo Press, 950 Parker St., Berkeley, CA 94710.

** In many states that accept holographic wills, they are valid if there is writing on them that is not all in the testator's handwriting, as long as that writing is not "material" i.e., does not affect the provisions of the will. To be safe, however, it is best to be sure everything in a holographic will is in your own writing.

*** The French philosopher Rabelais left a will of admirable simplicity. It reads in its entirety: "I have nothing. I owe a great deal. The rest I give to the poor."

## Last Will and Testament

I, Felix Finnegan, declare this to be my Last Will and Testament. I revoke all prior wills and codicils:

First: I am not now married. My marriage to Loretta Jones Finnegan was terminated by divorce on October 3, 1977 by the Superior Court of the State of California, County of Alameda, Case #00000. I deliberately make no provision for my former wife in my will. I have two children, Susie Jones Finnegan and Felix Finnegan, Jr. also known as Junior Finnegan. I deliberately make no provision for my children in my will. *

Second: I leave my collection of bumper stickers to the Berkeley Public Library.

Third: I leave my dog, Beagle, to Delilah Kimura, who resides at 1137 Penn Street, Oakland, California.

Fourth: I leave my 350 cc Honda motorcycle to Ruth More, who resides at 1143 Penn Street, Oakland, California. **

---

* In some states if you fail to mention children or spouses in your will, there is a presumption that you left them out inadvertently and that they should receive a share anyway (this is especially true for children and spouses who came along after the will was written). So keep your will up-to-date and specifically state that you don't want to leave them anything if that is your plan. Specifically mention all children you plan to disinherit. In order to disinherit children it is usually not sufficient to have a will saying only that they are disinherited. If you don't make a provision for what will become of your property instead, they will take anyway under the intestate succession laws. If you are divorced, give the date and court number of your divorce judgement in disinheriting your ex-spouse. This will avoid any confusion about whether you're actually still married. In some states, a spouse gets a forced share of the property even if disinherited by name. If you are still married to someone that you don't want to share in your property, and for some reason can't get a divorce, it might be best to research the laws of your state and if necessary consult a lawyer to find an alternative estate plan.

** In this will we assume that you are leaving only small amounts of property, having taken care of more major items in other ways so as to avoid probate. As long as you are only willing a dog, or teacups, or a motorcycle or a little furniture, your will won't be probated. However, if you are using a will to leave property worth **more** than $10,000–$50,000 (depending on the state), your will is likely to result in a probate proceeding and you will want to guard against the danger that a person who inherits under the will may die before your probate is completed. If this happens, your property will go to that person's heirs and will have to go through probate twice. To avoid this, you can include the following clause: "To inherit under the terms of this will, a person must survive me by 180 days. If he/she does not, the property left that person shall pass under the terms of the remainder clause of this will which is paragraph _____ ."

Fifth: I leave the remainder of my estate to my companion of many years, Keija Adams. If she is not then living, I leave the remainder of my property to my parents, Herbert Finnegan and Mary Finnegan, in equal shares. If my parents do not survive me, I leave the remainder of my property to the American Civil Liberties Union of Northern California.

Sixth: I nominate Keija Adams as executrix of my will. If she is not then living I nominate Delilah Kimura to act in her place. I direct that no bond be required of my executrix.

Executed at Berkeley, California
on February 23, 1984

Felix Finnegan

## E. AVOIDING PROBATE

Probate is commonly a good thing to avoid. The probate of a will involves statutory fees that are often substantial.

As mentioned above, passing property by will won't avoid probate in most states except where small amounts of property are concerned ($10,000-$50,000 depending on the state). To avoid the time, expense and court appearances involved in probating a will, more and more people are transferring assets at death by other means. We don't have space for a comprehensive discussion of all probate-avoiding devices here, but the following are some of the commonest.

### 1. Joint Tenancy

This has been discussed in Chapter 7; briefly, not only real property, but bank accounts, automobiles, savings bonds, stocks and other items may be owned jointly so that when one "joint tenant" dies, the other joint tenant owns the whole asset without the necessity of disposing of it in a will.*As a matter of fact, if two persons own an asset in joint tenancy, one person will own the whole asset upon the other person's death, even if the deceased person tried to dispose of his share in a will.

### 2. Life Insurance

You should name a living individual as your beneficiary and a contingent beneficiary who will take the proceeds if the primary beneficiary is not living at the time of your death. You do not want the benefits paid into your estate, which is what will happen if there is no living beneficiary. Paying money into your estate will necessitate court action, whereas proceeds of a life insurance policy will ordinarily be paid to the beneficiary without regard to the terms of the deceased person's will, and without court probate proceedings. There are often substantial tax savings if you give the policy to the beneficiary. See *Planning Your Estate*, Clifford, Nolo Press.

### 3. Trusts

There are two basic types of trusts, "inter-vivos" trusts, and testamentary trusts (those created by wills). A revocable inter-vivos trust (commonly called a "living trust"; the Latin means "among the living") is essentially a paper transaction designed solely to avoid probate. You appoint yourself trustee, transfer property to the trust (assets of your business, say) and name the beneficiary (your lover). While you live, you retain full ownership of the house. You can revoke the trust at any time.

Creation of a probate-avoidance, inter-vivos trust need not require complicated legal work; simple, standard-form trusts can be used (you will find a sample in the Appendix). If you do establish such a trust, be sure you understand the paperwork

---

* In a few states such as Texas, joint tenancy is not an efficient way to pass property. If you are using joint tenancy to pass large amounts of property be sure you understand the law in your state.

required, keep accurate records, and actually transfer the trust property. (If real property is placed in the trust, the transfer of the property should be recorded with the local Recorder's Office).

Testamentary trusts are usually desirable only for large estates (over $500,000) and are most commonly used to save on taxes. Because of the complicated nature of this legal area, a serious discussion of these trusts is beyond the scope of this book. But if you do have a substantial estate, you may well save considerable death taxes by the use of testamentary trusts, particularly if you fit into one of the following situations. If so, see a tax accountant.

• If the bulk of your estate will be left to a person who is old or ill and likely to die soon, when that person dies, the money and property you left him or her will again be subject to death taxes. Estate planners call this the "second" tax. If you establish a testamentary trust leaving the old or ill person only the income from the trust, this "second tax" can be avoided.

• If you leave all your money to your children (and grandchildren), it will be taxed when you die and then taxed again when your children die. For years, one of the death tax dodges of the very rich was to leave their wealth in trust for their grandchildren, escaping taxation on the middle generation. The 1976 Tax Reform Act supposedly curtailed this by introducing the notion of a "generation-skipping transfer." In essence, the tax laws now state that a person can leave a maximum of $250,000 per child (not per grandchild) in a death-tax-free trust. Any amount over the $250,000 limit per child is subject to regular federal estate taxes. So if you have three children (and a passel of grandchildren), and a hunk of money, you may want to establish three separate $250,000 generation-skipping trusts. If so, you'll need to see a lawyer.

**NOTE:** Most kinds of trusts are cumbersome and involve a fair amount of paperwork. However, there is one kind of trust that may suit your needs even if you are not wealthy. This is an informal bank trust account which is held as follows: "Keija Adams, Trustee for Felix Finnegan." On the death of Keija, Felix owns the entire account. However, while both parties are living, only Keija has access to the account. Your local bank can help you set up this kind of trust account.

### 4. United States Savings Bonds

If you own such bonds (which are **not** a very good investment if you are concerned with the rate of return on your money), you can register them in your name with the further designation "P.O.D. (Pay on Death) to <u>name of beneficiary</u>". You can change the beneficiary at any time without the beneficiary's permission and, at your death, the bonds will then be payable to the designated bereficiary without the need for any court proceedings.

### 5. Miscellaneous Benefits

Many people are covered by Social Security, Veterans Benefits, Railroad Pensions and various other pension and/or retirement plans. Under most of these plans you have no right to any benefits if the person with whom you have been living dies. This is true of the government plans and many private plans. You should check to see if your private plan allows you to name a beneficiary. If this is the case, you should immediately do so. You can always change your beneficiary, but if you do not have one, it may end up that no one gets your benefits and they will go back into the company. No matter how many promises you and your partner made to each other, and no matter how much you were dependent on his or her income to exist, if you want to partake in any of these plans, you must be named in writing. Otherwise, you have no rights in the event of the death of your partner.

**REVIEW NOTE:** How to dispose of your estate depends mainly upon how much (and what) you have and your relations with the persons close to you. However, one word of caution: **If you have been living with someone for a long time, do not assume that you have been provided for. Ask** your partner if he or she has a will, and check how your assets are owned. If you and your friend do not make preparations ahead of time, one of you may find himself/herself left with nothing, even though this is not what was intended. There is no reason to let mean old Tillie in Omaha have a cent if you do even a little planning.

## F. AVOIDING DEATH TAXES

You will remember that in Chapter 3 we discussed the fact that there are often income tax incentives to live together as opposed to getting married. Unfortunately this is one time where what is true in life isn't true in death. Under the federal estate tax rules and under the inheritance tax laws of many states it is far cheaper to die married.* Why? Because large chunks of money can be passed from one spouse to the other with no taxation at all, but these tax preferences are not available to unmarried couples. So if one unmarried partner is very ill or very old and that person has a substantial amount of money that he or she wishes to leave the other, check out the inheritance and estate tax tables. It is very possible that you will conclude that marriage makes great economic sense. You can marry up until the day you die and still qualify for the marital exemption.

## G. PROVIDING FOR YOUR KIDS BY WILL

There isn't a whole lot we can do to protect our children even if we are model parents. In the last analysis, they are responsible for making their own destiny. Still, we worry that if we die, things will be hard for them and we hope that we can make plans now that will ease their way if we are no longer here. It is particularly necessary that we do this for children born outside of marriage as these children may not be

---

* All property left to a surviving spouse is exempt from federal estate taxes.

included under the intestate succession laws of some states. Legal problems tend to fall into two broad areas: support and custody.

If property is being left to a child, it is very common to name a "guardian of the estate" in the will.* The guardian of the estate manages and controls the property inherited by or otherwise owned by the minor, but has no right to custody. Guardians of the estate are quite common and are frequently used even if the other parent is living. This is especially true if you have a trusted friend or relative who is knowledgeable about money matters, and the other parent is not. To appoint a guardian of the estate of a minor, you can use language like this in your will:

*"At my death, if any of my children are minors, I appoint __(name of guardian)__ of_____(address)_____as guardian of the estate of my minor child or children. If he/she shall for any reason fail to qualify or cease to act as such guardian, I appoint _____(name)_____ as such guardian in his/her place."*

People are often more concerned about the custody of their children if they suddenly die than they are with financial matters. It is common, for example, that a divorced parent who is living with someone will want that person rather than the other parent to have custody. Indeed, it is a common misconception that people can "will" their children to someone other than the natural parent. This cannot be done if the natural parent has been visiting and supporting his or her child unless the parent is obviously unfit. The law of every state strongly favors the interests of natural parents over everyone else (see Chapters 8 and 9). However, if the other parent is not living or his (her) whereabouts are not known, or he (she) has no interest in the child and will not attempt to obtain custody, it is possible to designate in a will the person whom you wish to be the guardian of the child should you die. In legal jargon this is known as a "testamentary guardianship" and the person who is named as the guardian is known as "guardian of the person" of the minor. Here is language which you can use in your will:

*"If at my death any of my children are minors, I appoint _____(name)_____ of _____(address)_____as guardian of the person of my minor child or children. If he/she shall for any reason fail to qualify or cease to act as such guardian, I appoint _____(name of successor)_____ of _____(address)_____to serve in his/her place."*

If a parent does name a testamentary guardian in his or her will, the court is not required to actually appoint this person as the guardian. However, the wishes of the parent are accorded great respect, and the court will usually appoint the person named in the will unless there is evidence showing that person is unfit.

---

* In thinking about providing for your children's financial future, don't forget that, if a wage earner dies, his dependent children are entitled to Social Security survivor's benefits.

** If any substantial amount of property is to be given to a minor it is important to do this under the terms of the Uniform Gifts to Minors Act. This can be done as follows, "To _____, an adult ____Californian or whatever_____, or appropriate _____(STATE)_____ financial institution as custodian for _____(NAME OF MINOR)_____ under the _____(STATE)_____Uniform Gift to Minors Act."

**NOTE:** Be realistic if you name someone as a guardian. Check to make sure the person is willing and able to assume custody of the child. Also be sure to keep this provision up-to-date. In an era of changing lifestyles and mobility, it is very difficult to predict the behavior and whereabouts of your friends throughout the minority of your child. Your sister and her husband may be very nice people, but ten years from now they may be divorced or living on a mountain top in Tibet. In most states a child of a certain age (typically 14) may nominate his own guardian and it may be better to give the choice to your child if he or she is of a suitable age.

## H. DEATH AND LIVING TOGETHER CONTRACTS

What does the *Marvin* and other palimony cases have to do with death? Nothing directly, but their implications are considerable. You will remember that in Chapters 4 and 5 we discussed the fact that in several states such as California, courts have not only made it clear that written contracts between unmarried couples are enforceable, but also have approved oral and implied contracts as well as several other equitable remedies. How does this relate to death, you say? Just be patient—we are getting to the point. Let's go back to the example at the beginning of this chapter involving the brick that falls on Felix's head and Aunt Tillie from Omaha who is as mean as a wounded rattlesnake and wants the $50,000 that Keija feels should rightly go to her. Remember, we told you that things didn't look good for Keija because Felix left no will, and under the "intestate succession" law, Tillie as the nearest relative inherits. This didn't seem to be fair (did it?) and you may have wondered if there isn't something that Keija can do.

Perhaps there is. Remember Keija and Felix were each saving money for their "joint future." Keija might claim that she and Felix had an oral contract to share all of their earnings.* If this were the case, then the money would belong to Keija. Of course, Keija would very likely have a hard time proving that an oral contract existed unless she had witnesses or some other documentation. Tillie would clearly claim that the fact that Keija and Felix kept their money in separate accounts was some evidence that they didn't mean to combine it.

We can't give you any hard and fast rules as to when the surviving member of an unmarried couple might be able to claim that a contract existed in order to get some of the deceased's estate if the deceased dies without a will. The courts have not yet made enough rulings in this area to have established guidelines. But if you are the survivor, you may have a case if any one of the following situations exist:

• You have been working in the home and your friend has been making the money. In many states you might be able to claim under an oral contract (if one existed and you could prove it). In a few states such as California, you might also

---

* In Chapters 4 and 5 we learned that oral living together contracts have been recognized by a number—but not all—states. Illinois and Maine are states where they are not recognized. In Georgia, even written contracts are not recognized.

attempt to claim all or part of the estate under an implied contract, or one or another equitable theory (see Chapter 4);

● You and your partner had been buying things and saving jointly and had agreed that all property belonged to both. Of course, you would have absolutely no trouble if you had followed our advice and written your agreement down, but even if your agreements were only oral, you may well be able to prove them (see Chapter 4);

● You and your partner jointly contribute to the purchase of real property, but for some reason the property was not put in "tenancy in common" or "joint tenancy," but only in the deceased's name. It is not easy to rebut the presumption that the person whose name is on the deed is the legal owner, but sometimes grounds necessary to establish an equitable remedy can be found (see Chapter 4).

**NOTE:** If your friend has died leaving no will or joint ownership provisions and you believe that you are entitled to inherit some or all of his or her property, see a lawyer immediately. There are a series of legal decisions in several states which have given relief to people in this situation.

## I. WHAT ABOUT MY BODY?

Most of us have no great attachment to our bodies once we take leave of them. Those of you who are into cryogenics (body freezing) and related body-saving techniques will have to look elsewhere for information. Here we are concerned only with those who are done with their bodies at death, not those who want to put them on the bedpost overnight for future use.

Many people make burial or cremation plans informally, trusting their families or friends to take care of the details after death. This works fine as long as you have confidence that your plans will be carried out. Often, however, there is a justifiable fear that your family will ignore your wishes after death, substituting their own. This is especially true if your blood relatives dislike the person you are living with.

If you are concerned about funeral arrangements, we suggest you do the following:

➋ Make practical arrangements for your funeral yourself. Get your burial plot or arrange for cremation, plan whatever ceremony you want and pay for it in advance;

➋ Leave instructions as part of your will. This can be done and is legal. You might include a provision in the will as follows: "*Upon my death I wish to be buried in the Little White Chapel Cemetary in Lancastershire, Massachusetts in plot number_____which is reserved and paid for (which will be paid for by my burial insurance through Carpenters Union 18). I wish no elaborate ceremony and wish my remains to be prepared for burial by the Fraternal Brothers Burial Society under the contract that I have signed with them. Any decisions not already made, or necessitated by circumstances that I cannot now foresee, I entrust to my friend of many years, Lucinda Whitehorse .*"

172

● Leave a letter of instructions in a place or with a person where it will be available immediately at your death. This letter should contain the same information about burial plans that is contained in your will. If your will is in a safe deposit box at your death, it may take several days to get it and a letter of instructions will be a great aid to family and friends.

**WARNING:** Do not leave a signed copy of your will in an accessible place. If a **signed** copy of your will is accidentally destroyed, in some states that will revoke the entire will. The instruction letter should contain only burial instructions and instructions as to where (i.e., safe deposit box) your actual will can be found.

awyers

St. Yves is from Brittany
A lawyer but not a thief.
Such a thing is beyond belief!*

Professionals of all sorts are in bad repute these days. There is a strong and often justifiable feeling that they hide behind knowing looks, mumbo jumbo and monopoly powers to charge high prices for what are often simple services. Lawyers are particularly guilty of this practice, for a great deal of what they do at $50 to $200 per hour amounts to little more than paper shuffling — paper shuffling that you can do simply and safely for yourself if you have the necessary information. Of course, keeping information hidden or obscured by funny sounding Latin and old-fashioned English terms is one way that lawyers protect their monopoly.

Does this mean that we don't think you should ever go near a lawyer? No. The fact that the legal system is riddled with abuse doesn't mean that you can completely avoid it. This book necessarily covers a lot of ground and may not be sufficiently detailed for all your purposes. You may need the information a lawyer has on some specific point or you may simply want an expert to check your work. What you want to do is use lawyers for your purposes, not theirs. Don't put yourself in the role of a passive "client".**Approach lawyers with a thorough knowledge of how they can help you and how much it will cost.

---

* Even in the middle ages lawyers allied themselves with the rich and powerful. This is part of a French poem about a lawyer who served the poor, which was such an unusual thing that he was made a saint. We discovered the quote in an excellent history of our legal system entitled Law And The Rise Of Capitalism, by Tigar and Levy: Monthly Review Press.
** In an interesting article entitled "Valuable Deficiencies, A Service Economy Needs People In Need," in the Fall 1977 Co-Evolution Quarterly, John McKnight Points out that "The Latin root of the word 'client' is a verb which translates 'to hear', 'to obey'."

## A. LAW LIBRARIES

Lawyers are experts at recycling information and charging enormous amounts for this limited service. We say limited because lawyers (or their para-legal assistants or secretaries) are often doing no more than opening a book of legal forms or information and copying out the answers. For example, if you want to process an adoption, change a name, get a divorce or accomplish most other legal tasks, the lawyer will do little more than fill in the boxes on pre-printed forms. Why can't you do this yourself? Often you can if you know which book to look in. They are all in your county law library which is free and open to the public (it ought to be as in most states your court filing fees pay for it).

The most important tool in your county law library is the annotated state codes. "Annotated" means that after each law is set out, there is a digest of excerpts from relevant judicial decisions and cross references to related articles and laws. The judicial decisions are kept in books that are arranged according to a simple code which your law librarian can quickly explain. Also, ask your librarian to show you any legal encyclopedia which explains your state laws. These are indexed by subject (you could look up cohabitation, child support, etc.) and are much like any other encyclopedia. You will want to check out the "Form" books. These are collections (often in many volumes) of sample legal forms designed to accomplish many thousands of legal tasks. Finally ask the law librarian if your state has a set of books designed to keep lawyers up-to-date. In California these are called CEB books and there is one covering every common area of law. There are also several national services in areas such as tax law, labor law, etc. As noted several times in this book, the one most relevant to you will probably be the Family Law Reporter. The best general guide to using the law library is Elias, *Legal Research: How to Find and Understand the Law*, Nolo Press.

## B. WHEN DO YOU NEED A LAWYER?

There is no simple answer to this question, but we can give you some suggestions:

### 1. Information

If after reading this book you feel you need more detailed information on a particular subject, a lawyer may be able to help you. Talking your problems over with a knowledgeable person may be all you need. You might, for example, want to know more about common law marriage rules or the tax consequences of setting up a trust. Because a great deal of this information is virtually inaccessible to the non-lawyer (hopefully this will change), lawyers may be your only resource. When making an appointment to get information from a lawyer, always observe rule one: find out in **advance** how much a consultation will cost.

### 2. Double-checking

You may feel that you have an excellent grasp on the legal aspects of a problem, but still feel that you want, and are willing to pay for, an expert opinion. A contract between you and your friend to buy a house is a good example of a situation where you might wish to have an attorney double-check your work. A will that involves considerable property is another. Where a lot is at stake, it never hurts to be a little extra careful. But be sure that the lawyer you approach is supportive of the idea that you intend to do most of the work yourself and that his or her role is that of a helper. Many lawyers resent people making their own decisions, so be wary.

### 3. Fighting In Court

The American judicial system is so slow, cumbersome, expensive, time-consuming and divorced from everyday reality, that we strongly urge you to avoid it if possible, even if this involves giving up some property or principles that are important to you. However, if you find yourself in court, whether in a property division or custody case or some other serious action, you should consult a lawyer. This doesn't mean that you should hire a lawyer to represent you. Most disputes that you are likely to become involved in are not difficult and representing yourself in court is not as hard as lawyers would like to pretend. Did you ever think that the old saying "a person who represents himself has a fool for a client" is such an old saying because lawyers have been brain-washing the public with it for generations. You want to find a lawyer who will help you to understand the procedures and issues involved. This can often be arranged for a fraction of the cost of turning the whole dispute over to a lawyer. Be sure your lawyer is willing to tell you how much he or she will charge in advance, what the charge is for. Remember, it's your case and your life, and you should be the one making the decisions.

### C. FINDING A LAWYER

Finding a lawyer who charges reasonable prices and who you feel can be trusted is not always an easy task. There is always the fear that by just picking a name out of the telephone book you may get someone unsympathetic, or perhaps an attorney who will charge too much. Certainly you have better things to do than talk to a lawyer who thinks that living together is a sleazy, sinful practice. You should realize that you are not the only one who feels a little scared and intimidated.

If you don't know an attorney who can be trusted and can't get a reliable recommendation from a friend, you have a problem. While you might be lucky and randomly pick an attorney who matches your needs perfectly, you might just as easily wind up paying too much for too little. Here are some suggestions that should make your search a little easier:

◗ Avoid referral panels set up by local bar associations. Any lawyer can get on these panels by paying a fee. While bar associations in some areas of the country make an effort to check that attorneys on their referral panels have expertise in their particular area, this is by no means a universal practice. You would often do as well to stick a pin in the Attorneys section of the phone book. Also, sticking a pin in the phone book is free whereas some of the reference panel systems will charge you as much as $25 for the referral;

176

◐ Check with a local consumer organization to see if they can recommend someone;

◐ Check the ads in the paper usually listed under "Business Personals" in the classified section. Often younger attorneys just starting out advertise low rates to build up a practice. Also, we know several semi-retired attorneys who advertise very reasonable rates for consultations with the understanding that they will not take cases to court. This could be just what you need.

◐ Shop around by calling different law offices and stating your problem. Ask them how much it would cost for a visit. Try to talk to a lawyer personally so you can get an idea of how friendly and sympathetic he is to your concerns. If you want advice on a specific area as opposed to turning your whole legal life over to the lawyer, make this clear from the beginning. Don't be afraid to fire a lawyer if you feel your problems are not getting sufficient attention. There will be 650,000 of them by 1985 and many are underemployed.

**EXAMPLE:** Let's think back to Chapter 7. Remember Keija and Felix and the contract they wrote when buying a house. This is the sort of agreement that they might want checked by a lawyer. As they have already done their homework, they should pay $75-$200 for this service depending on the complexity of their agreement. But, if instead of doing most of the work themselves, Keija and Felix simply call up the first lawyer someone suggests and show up at his or her office with a confused mish-mash of facts and hopes, they can expect to pay the lawyer a big chunk of cash (say $500-$1,000) to sort it out. This is assuming, of course, that the lawyer is sympathetic to start with. One couple called us recently and said that, after listening to their problems (which weren't difficult), a lawyer who was a friend of their parents made a pyramid of his fingers, cleared his throat, looked wise and told them "get married." Two days later a bill arrived for $100.

● Younger attorneys are probably going to be more sympathetic and knowledgeable about the problems of people living together than are their older colleagues. Remember, lawyers whose offices and lifestyles are reasonably simple are more likely to help you for less money than lawyers who feel naked unless wearing a $900 outfit. You should be able to find someone to help you for $50-$75 per hour. **Anything more is excessive.**

● When talking to the lawyer on the phone, or at the first conference, ask some specific questions. If the lawyer answers them clearly and concisely — explaining, but not talking down to you — fine. If he or she acts wise, but says little except to ask that the problem be placed in his or her hands (with the appropriate fee, of course), watch out. You are either talking with someone who doesn't know the answer and won't admit it (common), or someone who finds it impossible to let go of the "me expert, you peasant" way of looking at the world (even more common).

# Appendix

# LIVING TOGETHER CONTRACT

BETWEEN _____

AND _____

We, _____

and _____
make this agreement to set out the rights and obligations of our joint living arrangement. It is our intention to follow this agreement in a spirit of good faith and cooperation. We agree as follows:

## ARTICLE I

We choose to live together outside the formal state regulations governing marriage and divorce. This is our free choice and desire and we specifically state that we do not intend our relationship to be interpreted as a common law marriage. We further state that we each make this agreement in consideration of the agreement of the other, and that the provision of sexual services by either of us is not the basis of this contract. We further state that this agreement will remain in full force and effect until such time as we separate, or change it with a subsequent written, signed agreement.

## ARTICLE II

We are each equal and independent people, willing and able to support ourselves. We will share our love and good energy, but we reject the idea that one of us should be dependent upon the other for support.

## ARTICLE III

We agree that all income, however derived, and any accumulations of property traceable to that income, belongs absolutely to the person who earns or otherwise acquires the income. At the time of signing this contract, we have each prepared a list of major items of property that each of us owns. This list is marked as Exhibit 1 and is attached to this contract and by this reference made a part of this contract. We shall update this list as it becomes necessary. Any and all joint purchases shall be made under the terms of Article VI below.

## ARTICLE IV

We agree that any gifts or inheritances that either of us receives shall be the separate property of that person. Should a gift or inheritance be made to us jointly, we shall consider that we own it in equal shares unless otherwise specified by the donor.

## ARTICLE V

We agree that the separate property of either of us can become the separate property of the other, or the joint property of both of us, only under the terms of a written agreement signed by the person whose separate property is to be reclassified.

## ARTICLE VI

We agree that each of us will keep our own money in our own separate bank accounts and that we shall not open joint bank or credit accounts. We each further agree to return any credit cards that are issued to both of us, and, in addition, not to make any purchases using the credit or credit cards of the other.

## ARTICLE VII

As set forth in Article III above, we will each individually own all property purchased with the money we individually earn or otherwise accumulate. However, from time to time it may be necessary or desirable for us to pool our money to buy some item. If this is done, we will make a separate written agreement to cover each particular item of property that we acquire jointly. These agreements shall be marked Exhibit 2 and shall be attached to and incorporated in this agreement. As part of each joint agreement, we shall include a clause providing for what happens to the property if we separate. If for some reason we fail to provide for the contingency of our separation, we agree to divide all jointly-owned property equally. If we can't agree as to an equal division we shall sell the jointly-owned property and equally divide all proceeds of the sale.

## ARTICLE VIII

We agree to share equally all monthly household expenses. This includes food, incidental supplies necessary to home maintenance, rent and utilities, not including long distance phone charges which shall be paid by the person making the call.

## ARTICLE IX

We each agree to own, insure and pay for the maintenance of our own motor vehicles. If at any time we wish to share ownership of a motor vehicle, we shall make a separate written agreement as to ownership under the terms of Article VII and shall have the fact of joint ownership recorded on the motor vehicle title slip.

## ARTICLE X

We do not at present jointly own any real property. Should we jointly buy a house, land in the country, investment property or any other real property, we agree that a copy of a deed to the property and any and all supplementary contracts or agreements covering the property shall be marked as Exhibit 3 and attached to this contract and that when this is done they shall be incorporated into this contract. We further agree that neither of us shall have any rights to, or financial interest in, any separate real property of the other, whether acquired before or after the signing of this contract, unless such interest is set forth in a written agreement signed by both parties to this contract.

## ARTICLE XI

We realize that our power to contract as far as children are concerned is limited by state law. With this knowledge, and in a spirit of cooperation and mutual respect, we wish to state the following as our agreement should we have children.

1) The father shall sign a written statement acknowledging that he is the father of our child(ren) within ten days after birth;

2) Our child(ren) shall be given the following last name _____ ;

3) We reject the idea that one of us should do most of the child care tasks while the other provides the income. We will do our best to jointly share in the many responsibilities involved in feeding, clothing, loving and disciplining our child(ren);

4) Because of the possible trauma our separation might cause our child(ren), we shall each make a good faith effort to participate in a jointly-agreed upon program of counseling before separation;

5) If we separate, we shall do our best to see that our child(ren) has/have a good and healthful environment in which to grow up. Specifically we agree to the following:

a) We will do our best to see that our child(ren) maintain a close and loving relationship with each of us;

b) We will share in the upbringing of our child(ren) and, on the basis of our respective abilities to pay , support them;

c) We will make a good faith effort to make all major decisions affecting the health and welfare of our child(ren) jointly;

d) Should circumstances dictate that our child(ren) should spend a greater portion of the year living with one of us than the other, the person who has actual physical custody shall be sensitive to the needs of the other to have generous rights of visitation and shall cooperate in all practical steps necessary to make visitation as easy as possible;

e) If after separation we have problems communicating as to the best interest or interests of our child(ren), we shall seek out help in the form of a jointly-agreed-upon program of counseling with the hope that we can work out our differences without having to take our problems to court;

f) At the death of either of us, our child(ren) shall be cared for and raised by the other whether or not we are living together at the time of the death.

## ARTICLE XII

We agree that either of us can end our agreement to live together at any time by simply ceasing to live with the other. If this is done, neither of us shall have any claim upon the other for money or support, except as provided for by the terms of this agreement pertaining to the division of jointly owned property (Article VII).

## ARTICLE XIII

We agree that from time to time this contract may be amended. All amendments shall be in writing and shal be signed by both of us.

## ARTICLE XIV

We further agree that if any court finds any portion of this contract to be illegal or otherwise unenforceable, that the rest of the contract is still valid and in full force.

## ARTICLE XV

We agree that any dispute arising out of this contract shall be arbitrated under the terms of this clause. If we both choose, we shall first try to resolve the dispute with the help of a mutually agreed-upon mediator(s). Otherwise, either one of us may: (1) initiate arbitration by making a written demand for arbitration, defining the dispute

and naming one arbitrator; (2) within five days from receipt of this notice, the other shall name the second arbitator; (3) the two named arbitrators shall within ten days name a third arbitrator; (4) within seven days an arbitration meeting will be held. Each of us may have counsel if we choose, and may present the evidence and witnesses pertinent; (5) the arbitrators shall make their decision within five days after the hearing. Their decision shall be in writing and shall be binding upon us; (6) if the person to whom the demand for arbitration is directed fails to respond within five days, the other must give an additional five days' written notice of his or her intent to proceed. If there is no response, the person initiating the arbitration may proceed with the arbitration before the arbitrator he or she has designated, and his/her award shall have the same force as if it had been settled by all three arbitrators.

Executed at _____

_____     _____
            Date                              Signature

_____     _____
            Date                              Signature

# EXHIBIT 1

The following personal property is the separate property of

_____

The following personal property is the separate property of

_____

# EXHIBIT 2

The following property is jointly-owned by both of us under the terms and in the proportions set forth:

# LIVING TOGETHER CONTRACT

BETWEEN _____

AND _____

We, _____

and _____
make this agreement to set out the rights and obligations of our joint living arrangement. It is our intention to follow this agreement in a spirit of good faith and cooperation. We agree as follows:

**ARTICLE I**

We choose to live together outside the formal state regulations governing marriage and divorce. This is our free choice and desire and we specifically state that we do not intend our relationship to be interpreted as a common law marriage. We further state that we each make this agreement in consideration of the agreement of the other, and that the provision of sexual services by either of us is not the basis of this contract. We further state that this agreement will remain in full force and effect until such time as we separate, or change it with a subsequent written, signed agreement.

**ARTICLE II**

From the date this contract is signed, we will share all of our income and property accumulated with that income without regard to which of us earns or otherwise receives it. This does not include inheritances or gifts made to one of us. These shall remain the separate property of the person receiving the gift or inheritance under the terms of Article IV.

**ARTICLE III**

At the time of signing this contract, we have each prepared a list of major items of property that each of us owns as separate property. This list is marked as Exhibit 1 and is attached to this contract and by this reference made a part of this contract. We shall update this list as it becomes necessary. All separate property of each of us, and any income earned by this property shall remain the separate property of its owner unless it is transferred to the other person, or to joint ownership under the terms of a written document.

**ARTICLE IV**

We agree that any gifts or inheritances that either of us receives shall be the separate property of that person. Should a gift or inheritance be made to us jointly, we shall consider that we own it in equal shares unless otherwise specified by the donor.

**ARTICLE V**

We agree to maintain such joint and separate bank accounts and joint and separate credit accounts as appear to be reasonable from time to time. We agree to consult

one another on all purchases whether for cash or credit which exceed $200 and to make a good faith effort not to overspend our account.

## ARTICLE VI

We agree to own, insure and pay for the maintenance of our own motor vehicles. If at any time we wish to share ownership of a motor vehicle, we shall make a separate written agreement as to ownership under and shall have the fact of joint ownership recorded on the motor vehicle title slip.

## ARTICLE VII

We do not at present jointly own any real property. Should we jointly buy a house, land in the country, investment property or any other real property, we agree that a copy of a deed to the property and any and all supplementary contracts or agreements covering the property shall be marked as Exhibit 3 and attached to this contract and that when this is done they shall be incorporated into this contract. We further agree that neither of us shall have any rights to, or financial interest in, any separate real property of the other, whether acquired before or after the signing of this contract, unless such interest is set forth in a written agreement signed by both parties to this contract.

## ARTICLE VIII

We realize that our power to contract as far as children are concerned is limited by state law. With this knowledge, and in a spirit of cooperation and mutual respect, we wish to state the following as our agreement should we have children.

1) The father shall sign a written statement acknowledging that he is the father of our child(ren) within ten days after birth;

2) Our child(ren) shall be given the following last name _____ ;

3) We reject the idea that one of us should do most of the child care tasks while the other provides the income. We will do our best to jointly share in the many responsibilities involved in feeding, clothing, loving and disciplining our child(ren);

4) Because of the possible trauma our separation might cause our child(ren), we shall each make a good faith effort to participate in a jointly-agreed upon program of counseling before separation;

5) If we separate, we shall do our best to see that our child(ren) has/have a good and healthful environment in which to grow up. Specifically we agree to the following:

a) We will do our best to see that our child(ren) maintain a close and loving relationship with each of us;

b) We will share in the upbringing of our child(ren) and, on the basis of our respective abilities to pay, support them ;

c) We will make a good faith effort to make all major decisions affecting the health and welfare of our child(ren) jointly;

d) Should circumstances dictate that our child(ren) should spend a greater portion of the year living with one of us than the other, the person who has actual physical custody shall be sensitive to the needs of the other to have generous rights of visitation and shall cooperate in all practical steps necessary to make visitation as easy as possible;

e) If after separation we have problems communicating as to the best interest or interests of our child(ren), we shall seek out help in the form of a jointly-agreed-upon program of counseling with the hope that we can work out our differences without having to take our problems to court;

f) At the death of either of us, our child(ren) shall be cared for and raised by the other whether or not we are living together at the time of the death.

## ARTICLE IX

We agree that either of us can terminate this agreement by simply choosing not to live with the other. Should this be done, all jointly-owned property shall be equally divided at the time of the separation. Neither of us will have any obligation to support the other afte separation.

## ARTICLE X

We agree that from time to time this contract may be amended. All amendments shall be in writing and shal be signed by both of us.

## ARTICLE XI

We further agree that if any court finds any portion of this contract to be illegal or otherwise unenforceable, that the rest of the contract is still valid and in full force.

## ARTICLE XII

We agree that any dispute arising out of this contract shall be arbitrated under the terms of this clause. If we both choose, we shall first try to resolve the dispute with the help of a mutually agreeable mediator(s). Otherwise, either one of us may: (1) initiate arbitration by making a written demand for arbitration, defining the dispute and naming one arbitrator; (2) within five days from receipt of this notice, the other shall name the second arbitator; (3) the two named arbitrators shall within ten days name a third arbitrator; (4) within seven days an arbitration meeting will be held. Each of us may have counsel if we choose, and may present the evidence and witnesses pertinent; (5) the arbitrators shall make their decision within five days after the hearing. Their decision shall be in writing and shall be binding upon us; (6) if the person to whom the demand for arbitration is directed fails to respond within five days, the other must give an additional five days' written notice of his or her intent to proceed. If there is no response, the person initiating the arbitration may proceed with the arbitration before the arbitrator he or she has designated, and his/her award shall have the same force as if it had been settled by all three arbitrators.

Executed at _____

_____     _____
Date                              Signature


_____     _____
Date                              Signature

# EXHIBIT 1

The following personal property is the separate property of

_____

The following personal property is the separate property of

_____

# EXHIBIT 2

The following property is jointly-owned by both of us under the terms and in the proportions set forth:

# Acknowledgement
# of Paternity

_____ hereby acknowledges that he is the natural father of _____,

born _____ to _____ in _____.

_____ further states that he has welcomed _____ into his

home and that it is his intention and belief that he has taken all steps necessary

to fully legitimate _____ for all purposes, including the right to inherit

from, and through him, at the time of his death.

_____ further expressly acknowledges his duty to properly raise

and adequately support _____.


_____          _____
DATE

# Power of Attorney

Know all persons by these presents that I, _____, a legal resident of _____, hereby appoint _____, whose present address is _____, my lawful attorney to act as follows:

I grant to my said attorney full and sole power to do and execute all or any of the following acts, deeds, or documents as fully as and in the place of any spouse, parent, or other relative.

1. To authorize my medical treatment if I shall be physically or mentally incapacitated or otherwise unable to make such authorization for myself, including authorization for emergency care, hospitalization, surgery, therapy and/or any other kind of treatment which he/she shall, in her/his sole discretion, think necessary.

2. To be given first priority in visitation should I be a patient in any institution and unable to express a preference on account of my illness or disability.

3. To receive into her/his possession any and all items of personal property and effects that may be recovered from or about my person by any hospital, police agency, or any other person at the time of my illness, disability, or death.

4. To authorize the release of my body from any hospital or any other authority having possession of my body at the time of my death and to make all decisions necessary for and incident to the removal and transportation of my body from the place of my death.

5. To make all decisions necessary for the performance of funeral and burial services, if any.

6. To have published in any newspaper an obituary notice containing whatever information he/she may choose.

7. To contract with any competent person or company for the rendering of professional services by any funeral director of his/her choosing.

8. To make all decisions necessary for the interment or cremation of my body, including but not limited to the selection of a casket or urn, selection of a grave site, and selection of a gravestone and the inscription thereon.

9. To contract with any person or company for the provision of care and tending of my grave site.

10. To execute all necessary instruments and to perform all necessary acts required for the execution and implementation of the aforesaid authorization.

IT IS MY EXPRESS INTENTION that no powers granted by this instrument shall be revoked, terminated, or otherwise limited in any manner whatsoever by my death or mental or physical incapacity. And I declare that any act lawfully done hereunder by my said attorney shall be binding on myself and my heirs, legal and personal representatives, and assigns.

In witness thereof, I have hereunto set my hand and seal this _____ day of _____, 19____.

_____

# Acknowledgement

:ss

I, _____, do hereby certify that I am a duly commissioned, qualified, and authorized notary public in and for the _____ of _____; and that _____, grantor in the foregoing Power of Attorney hereto annexed, who is personally well known to me as the person who executed the foregoing Power of Attorney, appeared before me this day within the territorial limits of my authority, and being first duly sworn executed said instrument after the contents thereof had been read and duly explained to her/him and acknowledged that the execution of said instrument by her/him was her/his free and voluntary act and deed for the uses and purposes therein set forth.

In witness whereof, I have hereunto set my hand and affixed my official seal this _____ day of _____, 19_____.


My commission expires

_____.

_____
(Notary Public)

# Declaration of Revocable Trust for Personal Property

**Section I  Trustees and Beneficiary**

(a) __(name of settlor)__ , called the "settlor" and/or the "trustee" declares that __he/she__ has set aside and holds in trust all that property described in Schedule A, attached to this trust instrument, for the use and benefit of __(beneficiary)__ . The trustee of this trust shall be __(name of settlor)__ . Upon my death the trustee of this trust shall be __(name and address)__ .*

Alternative paragraph I(a) — if settlor is **not** trustee:

(a) __(name of settlor)__ , the "settlor" declares that __he/she__ has transferred to this trust all that property described in Schedule A, attached to this trust instrument, for the use and benefit of __(beneficiary)__ . The trustee of this trust shall be __(trustee's name and address)__ .

(b) Each person designated or acting as a trustee of any trust shall have the power to designate successor trustees to act when he or she shall become unable or unwilling to act as trustee of the trust. Each person may designate the same or different persons or entities, including corporate fiduciaries, to act as successor trustee of the trust. If all individuals appointed as trustee and any successors designated by them shall be unable or unwilling to act as trustees __(name successor trustee, possibly a bank)__ shall act as trustee. Any person acting as trustee of the trust may revoke any previous designation of any successor to himself; and appoint other successor trustees; all such revocations or designations shall be made in writing and are effective on delivery of the writing to __(person selected, normally a beneficiary of the trust)__ .

(c) All trustees shall serve without bond.

**Section II  The Trust Estate**

(a) The property subject to this intervivos trust, as listed in Schedule A, is referred to as the "trust estate" and shall be held, administered, and distributed in accordance with this instrument.

---

* I strongly advise you select a person you trust to be successor trustee, and do not select a bank or other large institution.

(b) Until the property listed in Schedule A is transferred to __(beneficiary)__ ,
pursuant to the terms of this trust, all income or profits which may accrue from said
property shall be distributed to the settlor during __(his/her)__ lifetime. (If community
property is transferred to the trust, specify whether a gift has been made from one spouse
to the other or not.)

## Section III   Transfer of Trust Property to Beneficiary

Upon my death, my successor trustee is hereby directed to transfer all property of this
trust to the beneficiary __(name)__ , alter payment of any debts, taxes or other
expenses incurred in connection with administration of this trust or trust property , and
thereby terminate this trust.

[If the beneficiary is a minor, add:]

If the beneficiary is under 18, the successor trustee shall hold the trust assets in trust,
under the California Uniform Gift to Minors Act, and administer the trust in the best
interests of __(name of beneficiary)__ .

## Section IV   Reserved Powers of Settlor

(a) I reserve unto myself the power to amend or revoke this intervivos trust, at any
time during my lifetime, without the necessity of obtaining the consent of the beneficiary.

(b) I reserve unto myself the power to name a new beneficiary, should _____
__(beneficiary)__, predecease me; should I fail to name a new beneficiary, following the death of
__(beneficiary)__ , this trust shall terminate on my death, and the trust property revert to
my estate (**or** if you wish to name further successor beneficiaries, do so here).

_____
(signature)

[have signature notarized; it's safer.]

Dated: _____

==================================================

## Schedule A – Property Transferred to Trust

[List all property transferred to this specific intervivos trust. List the property with
detail, e.g., if real estate is transferred to the trust, identify that real estate as it is identified
on the property ownership deed. Be sure to staple this schedule to the trust document.
Be sure to clarify exactly what property is in the trust — e.g. if community property is
placed in it, state whether your spouse's interest is also put in that trust, or whether, as is
usual, only your share of the community property is transferred. And if there is a formal
ownership document for trust property, as for a car, house, stocks, be sure to register the
trust as the legal owner of that property on a new ownership document.]

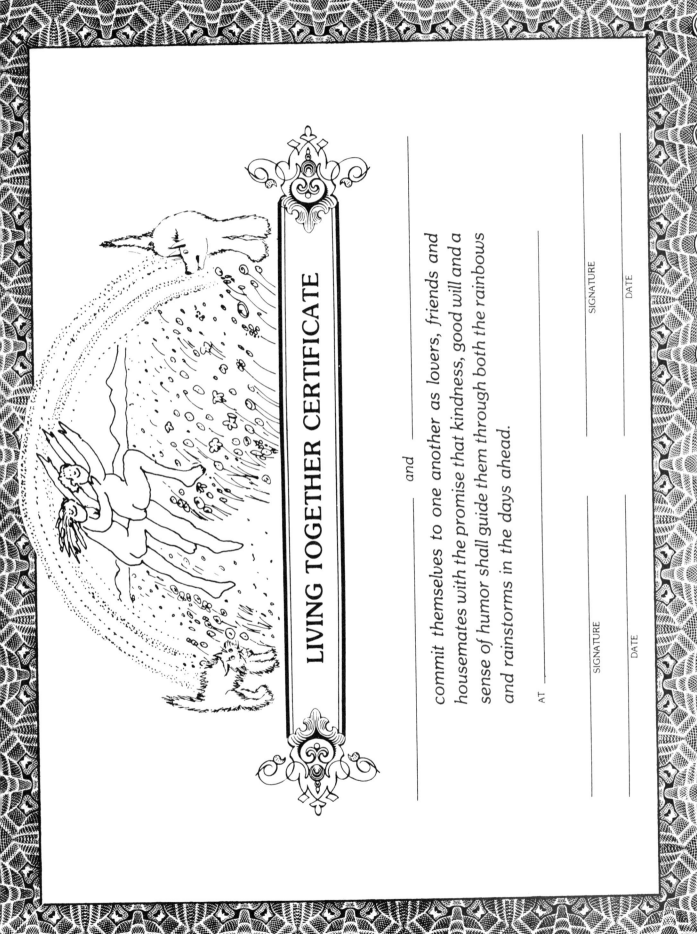

# LIVING TOGETHER CERTIFICATE

_____ and _____

commit themselves to one another as lovers, friends and housemates with the promise that kindness, good will and a sense of humor shall guide them through both the rainbows and rainstorms in the days ahead.

AT _____

_____
SIGNATURE

_____
DATE

_____
SIGNATURE

_____
DATE

## ABOUT RALPH

Ralph is the leader of the "do your own law" movement on the West Coast. As a co-founder of Nolo Press and the author of numerous books and articles aimed at giving the non-lawyer so-called "legal information" to deal with their own life decisions, he has constantly tried to expand the areas in which people can help themselves.

Ralph has a license to practice law. He doesn't use it. Instead, he gives lectures and workshops on such subjects as "Law for Unmarried Couples," "Tenants' Rights," and "How to Use Small Claims Court." He is the author of ten books on law including *29 Reasons Not to Go to Law School* which he co-authored with Toni. Ralph lives in Berkeley with Toni and three freckled Japanese goldfish.

## ABOUT TONI

Toni is an anthropologist turned lawyer turned graphic artist. She is the co-author and illustrator of *The Treasure of Lost Dragon Castle*, as well as several self-help law books, including *California Marriage and Divorce Law*. Toni is an original member of the Nolo Press family and has been involved in the people's law movement since its inception. Her articles have appeared in *New West*, *MS* and *Harper's Bazaar*.

## UPDATE SERVICE & LEGAL DIRECTORY

Our books are as current as we can make them, but sometimes the laws do change between editions. You can read about any law changes which may affect this book in the **NOLO NEWS**, a 12 page newspaper which we publish quarterly.

In addition to the **Update Service**, each issue contains a directory of people-oriented lawyers and legal clinics available to answer questions, handle a complicated case or process your paperwork at a reasonable cost. Also featured are comprehensive articles about the growing self-help law movement as well as areas of the law that are sure to affect you.

To receive the next 4 issues of the **NOLO NEWS**, please send us $2.00.

Name_____

Address _____

_____

Send to: **NOLO PRESS, 950 Parker St., Berkeley, CA 94710**

# BUSINESS & FINANCE

## How To Form Your Own California Corporation

By attorney Anthony Mancuso. Provides you with all the forms, Bylaws, Articles, minutes of meeting, stock certificates and instructions necessary to form your small profit corporation in California. It includes a thorough discussion of the practical and legal aspects of incorporation, including the tax consequences.
California Edition.                    $21.95

## The Non-Profit Corporation Handbook

By attorney Anthony Mancuso. Completely updated to reflect all the new law changes effective January 1980. Includes all the forms, Bylaws, Articles, minutes of meeting, and instructions you need to form a nonprofit corporation in California. Step-by-step instructions on how to choose a name, draft Articles and Bylaws, attain favorable tax status. Thorough information on federal tax exemptions which groups outside of California will find particularly useful.
California Edition                     $19.95

## The California Professional Corporation Handbook

By attorneys Mancuso and Honigsberg. In California there are a number of professions which must fulfill special requirements when forming a corporation. Among them are lawyers, dentists, doctors and other health professionals, accountants, certain social workers. This book contains detailed information on the special requirements of every profession and all the forms and instructions necessary to form a professional corporation.                    $21.95

## Billpayers' Rights

By attorneys Honigsberg & Warner. Complete information on bankruptcy, student loans, wage attachments, dealing with bill collectors and collection agencies, credit cards, car repossessions, homesteads, child support and much more.
California Edition                     $10.95

## The Partnership Book

By attorneys Clifford & Warner. When two or more people join to start a small business, one of the most basic needs is to establish a solid, legal partnership agreement. This book supplies a number of sample agreements with the information you will need to use them as is or to modify them to fit your needs. Buy-out clauses, unequal sharing of assets, and limited partnerships are all discussed in detail.
California Edition          $15.95
National Edition           $15.95

## Plan Your Estate: Wills, Probate Avoidance, Trusts & Taxes

By attorney Clifford. Comprehensive information on making a will, alternatives to probate, planning to limit inheritance and estate taxes, living trusts, and providing for family and friends. An explanation of the new statutory will and usable, tear-out forms are included.
California Edition                     $15.95

## Chapter 13: The Federal Plan To Repay Your Debts

By attorney Janice Kosel. This book allows an individual to develop and carry out a feasible plan to pay his or her debts in whole over a three-year period. Chapter 13 is an alternative to straight bankruptcy and yet it still means the end of creditor harassment, wage attachments and other collection efforts. Comes complete with all the forms and worksheets you need.
National Edition                      $12.95

## Bankruptcy: Do-It-Yourself

By attorney Janice Kosel. Tells you exactly what bankruptcy is all about and how it affects your credit rating, your property and debts, with complete details on property you can keep under the state and federal exempt property rules. Shows you step-by-step how to do it yourself and comes with all forms and instructions necessary.
National Edition                      $12.95

## Legal Care for Software

By Dan Remer.  Here we show the software programmer how to protect his/her work through the use of trade secret, trade-work, copyright, patent and, most especially, contractual laws and agreements. This book is full of forms and instructions that give programmers the hands-on information to do it themselves.
National Edition                    $24.95

## We Own It!

By C.P.A.s Kamoroff and Beatty and attorney Honigsberg.  This book provides the legal, tax and management information you need to start and successfully operate all types of coops and collectives.                           $ 9.00

# FAMILY & FRIENDS

## How To Do Your Own Divorce

By attorney Charles Sherman.  Now in its tenth edition, this is the original "do your own law" book.  It contains tear-out copies of all the court forms required for an uncontested dissolution, as well as instructions for certain special forms--military waiver, pauper's oath, lost summons, and publications of summons.
California Edition                   $ 9.95
Texas Edition                       $ 9.95

## California Marriage & Divorce Law

By attorneys Ihara and Warner.  This book contains invaluable information for married couples and those considering marriage on community and separate property, names, debts, children, buying a house, etc.  Includes sample marriage contracts, a simple will, probate avoidance information and an explanation of gift and inheritance taxes.  Discusses "secret marriage" and "common law" marriage.  California Edition        $14.95

## How To Adopt Your Stepchild

By Frank Zagone.  Shows you how to prepare all the legal forms; includes information on how to get the consent of the natural parent and how to conduct an "abandonment" proceeding.  Discusses appearing in court, making changes in birth certificates.
California Edition                   $14.95

## Small-Time Operator

By Bernard Kamoroff, C.P.A.  Shows you how to start and operate your small business, keep your books, pay your taxes and stay out of trouble.  Comes complete with a year's supply of ledgers and worksheets designed especially for small businesses, and contains invaluable information on permits, licenses, financing, loans, insurance, bank accounts, etc.  Published by Bell Springs Press.  National Edition  $ 8.95

## SOURCEBOOK FOR OLDER AMERICANS

By attorney Joseph Matthews.  The most comprehensive resource tool on the income, rights & benefits of Americans over 55. Includes detailed information on social security, retirement rights, Medicare, Medicaid, supplemental security income, private pensions, age discrimination, as well as a thorough explanation of the new social security legislation.
National Edition                    $10.95

## A Legal Guide for Lesbian/Gay Couples

By attorneys Hayden Curry and Denis Clifford.  Here is a book that deals specifically with legal matters of lesbian and gay couples.  Discusses areas such as raising children (custody, support, living with a lover), buying property together, wills, etc. and comes complete with sample contracts and agreements.  National Edition       $14.95

## After The Divorce: How To Modify Alimony, Child Support and Child Custody

By attorney Joseph Matthews.  Detailed information on how to increase alimony or child support, decrease what you pay, change custody and visitation, oppose modifications by your ex.  Comes with all the forms and instructions you need. Sections on joint custody, mediation, and inflation.
California Edition                   $14.95

## The Living Together Kit

By attorneys Ihara and Warner.  A legal guide for unmarried couples with information about buying or sharing property, the Marvin decision, paternity statements, medical emergencies and tax consequences.  Contains a sample will and Living Together Contract.
National Edition                    $14.95

## The People's Law Review

Edited by Ralph Warner. This is the first compendium of people's law resources ever published. It celebrates the coming of age of the self-help law movement and contains a 50-state catalog of self-help law materials; articles on mediation and the new "non-adversary" mediation centers; information on self-help law programs and centers (programs for tenants, artists, battered women, the disabled, etc.); articles and interviews by the leaders of the self-help law movement, and articles dealing with many common legal problems which show people "how to do it themselves" without lawyers. National Edition $ 8.95

## Author Law

By attorney Brad Bunnin and Peter Beren. A comprehensive explanation of the legal rights of authors. Covers contracts with publishers of books and periodicals, with sample contracts provided. Explains the legal responsibilities between co-authors and with agents, and how to do your own copyright. Discusses royalties negotiations, libel, and invasion of privacy. Includes a glossary of publishing terms. $14.95

## The Criminal Records Book

By attorney Siegel. Takes you step-by-step through all the procedures available to get your records sealed, destroyed or changed. Detailed discussion on: your criminal record--what it is, how it can harm you, how to correct inaccuracies, marijuana possession records & juvenile court records. Complete with forms and instructions. $12.95

## Legal Research: How To Find and Understand The Law

By attorney Steve Elias. A hands-on guide to unraveling the mysteries of the law library. For paralegals, law students, consumer activists, legal secretaries, business and media people. Shows exactly how to find laws relating to specific cases or legal questions, interpret statutes and regulations, find and research cases, understand case citations and Shepardize them. National Edition $12.95

## California Tenants' Handbook

By attorneys Moskovitz, Warner & Sherman. Discusses everything tenants need to know in order to protect themselves: getting deposits returned, breaking a lease, getting repairs made, using Small Claims Court, dealing with an unscrupulous landlord, forming a tenants' organization, etc. Completely updated to cover new rent control information and law changes for 1981. Sample Fair-to-Tenants lease and rental agreements. California Edition $ 9.95

## Everybody's Guide to Small Claims Court

By attorney Ralph Warner. Guides you step-by-step through the Small Claims procedure, providing practical information on how to evaluate your case, file and serve papers, prepare and present your case, and, most important, how to collect when you win. Separate chapters focus on common situations (landlord-tenant, automobile sales and repair, etc.). $ 9.95

## Fight Your Ticket

By attorney David Brown. A comprehensive manual on how to fight your traffic ticket. Radar, drunk driving, preparing for court, arguing your case to a judge, cross-examining witnesses are all covered. California Edition $12.95

## Homestead Your House

By attorney Warner. Under the California Homestead Act, you can file a Declaration of Homestead and thus protect your home from being sold to satisfy most debts. This book explains this simple and inexpensive procedure and includes all the forms and instructions. Contains information on exemptions for mobile homes and houseboats. California Edition $ 8.95

## How To Change Your Name

By David Loeb. Changing one's name is a very simple procedure. Using this book, people can file the necessary papers themselves, saving $200-300 in attorney's fees. Comes complete with all the forms and instructions necessary for the court petition method or the simpler usage method. California Edition $14.95

## Marijuana: Your Legal Rights

By attorney Richard Moller. Here is the legal information all marijuana users and growers need to guarantee their constitutional rights and protect their privacy and property. Discusses what the laws are, how they differ from state to state, and how legal loopholes can be used against smokers and growers.
National Edition                    $9.95

## The Unemployment Benefits Handbook

By attorney Peter Jan Honigsberg. Comprehensive information on how to find out if you are eligible for benefits, how the amount of those benefits will be determined. It shows how to file and handle an appeal if benefits are denied and gives important advice on how to deal with the bureaucracy and the people at the unemployment office.
National Edition                    $ 5.95

## How To Become A United States Citizen

By Sally Abel. Detailed explanation of the naturalization process. Includes step-by-step instructions from filing for naturalization to the final oath of allegiance. Includes study guide on U.S. history & government. Text is written in both English & Spanish. $9.95

## Don't Sit In The Draft

By Charles Johnson. A draft counseling guide with information on how the system works, classifications, deferments, exemptions, medical standards, appeals and alternatives.
National Edition                    $ 6.95

## Landlording

By Leigh Robinson. Written for the conscientious landlord or landlady, this comprehensive guide discusses maintenance and repairs, getting good tenants, how to avoid evictions, recordkeeping, and taxes. Published by Express Press.
National Edition                    $15.00

## Write, Edit & Print

By Donald McCunn. Word processing with personal computers. A complete how-to manual including: evaluation of equipment, 4 fully annotated programs, operating instructions, sample application. 525 pages.                    $24.95

## Computer Programming for The Complete Idiot

By Donald McCunn. An excellent introduction to computers. Hardware and software are explained in everyday language and the last chapter gives information on creating original programs.
                                    $6.95

## California Dreaming: The Political Odyssey or Pat and Jerry Brown

By Roger Rapoport. Here for the first time is the story of the First Family of California Politics from the Gold Rush to the 1980s. Based on more than 200 interviews, access to papers previously unavailable to scholars, lengthy talks and travels with Pat and Jerry Brown and their family.                    $ 9.95

## 29 Reasons Not To Go To Law School

A humorous and irreverent look at the dubious pleasures of going to law school. By attorneys Ihara and Warner with contributions by fellow lawyers and illustrations by Mari Stein.    $ 4.95

# Order Form

| QUANTITY | TITLE | UNIT PRICE | TOTAL |
|----------|-------|------------|-------|
|          |       |            |       |
|          |       |            |       |
|          |       |            |       |
|          |       |            |       |
|          |       |            |       |
|          |       |            |       |
|          |       |            |       |
|          |       |            |       |
|          |       |            |       |
|          |       |            |       |
|          |       |            |       |
|          |       |            |       |
|          |       |            |       |
|          |       |            |       |
|          |       |            |       |
|          |       |            |       |
|          |       |            |       |
|          |       |            |       |

Prices subject to change

☐ Please send me a
   catalogue of your books

Tax: (California only) 6½% for Bart,
     Los Angeles, San Mateo & Santa
     Clara counties; 6% for all others

Name_____

Address_____

_____

SUBTOTAL _____

Tax _____

Postage & Handling __$1.00__

TOTAL _____

Send to:

NOLO PRESS
950 Parker St.
Berkeley, CA 94710